CHANTRY
CHAPELS
AND MEDIEVAL STRATEGIES
FOR THE AFTERLIFE

CHANTRY CHAPELS

AND MEDIEVAL STRATEGIES FOR THE AFTERLIFE

SIMON ROFFEY

TEMPUS

I dedicate this book to my children:
Iris, who was born at the beginning
and Gene who arrived at the end.
And to Ruby.

First published 2008

The History Press
Cirencester Road, Chalford,
Stroud, Gloucestershire, GL6 8PE
www.thehistorypress.co.uk

Tempus Publishing is an imprint of The History Press

British Library Cataloguing in Publication Data.
A catalogue record for this book is available from the British Library.

ISBN 978 0 7524 4571 7

Typesetting and origination by The History Press
Printed in Great Britain

CONTENTS

LIST OF ILLUSTRATIONS   7
ACKNOWLEDGEMENTS   13

1   INTRODUCTION   15
     A strategy for the medieval afterlife   18
     Chantries and late medieval religious practice: vision and memory   19
     Short-term and long-term strategies for the afterlife   21

2   PERSPECTIVES ON THE STUDY OF MEDIEVAL CHANTRY CHAPELS   23
     Traditional and historical perspectives on the medieval chantry   23
     Sources and approaches   25

3   THE AFTERLIFE AND THE ANGLO-SAXON CHURCH: 31
     THE FOUNDATIONS OF MEMORIAL PRACTICE
     Pre-Christian memorial practice in Anglo-Saxon England   31
     'Purgatory' and the Anglo-Saxon church   33
     The porticus: a context for commemoration?   36
     Intercession and the local church in Anglo-Norman England   42
     The local church in the twelfth century   44

4   LATE MEDIEVAL STRATEGIES FOR INTERCESSION   51
     Purgatory and burial custom   52
     Late medieval visions of the afterlife   55

5   THE FORM AND FABRIC OF CHANTRY CHAPELS IN RELIGIOUS HOUSES   61
    Accommodation   65
    Form and fabric   66
    Colleges   77
    Hospitals and almshouses   86

6   THE FORM AND FABRIC OF CHANTRY CHAPELS IN THE PARISH   89
    Introduction   89
    Bridges, walls, gates and houses   89
    The Parish church   94
    Parish guilds   106
    Parish chantry chapels: art and architecture   108

7   THE SPATIAL ARCHITECTURE OF MEDIEVAL CHANTRY CHAPELS   119
    Chantry chapels: privatised monuments in the wider context 119
    Saints' shrines and chantry chapel location   124
    Chantry chapels and the high altar   128
    Chantry chapels and processional routes   132
    Chantry chapels and public visibility   134
    Chantries, chapels and visual topography   136
    Visual relationships and chapel topography   139
    A 'spiritual network': chapels, chantries and the parish church 150
    Tombs and memorials   154
    Tombs as 'presencing mechanisms'   164

8   THE REFORMATION OF CHANTRY CHAPELS   167
    A lingering tradition?   174
    Post-Script: a revival of tradition   177

9   CONCLUSIONS   181

    SELECT BIBLIOGRAPHY AND FURTHER READING   185
    GENERAL INDEX   189
    INDEX OF PLACES   191

LIST OF ILLUSTRATIONS

1   Medieval wall painting, South Leigh, depicting St Michael and the Virgin Mary 'tipping the scales'

2   Early sixteenth-century Lamb chapel, Devizes

3   Anglo-Saxon church, Breamore

4   St Oswald's Gloucester, showing conjectural location of altar

5   St Laurence, Bradford-on-Avon, showing conjectural location of altar

6   St Apôtres, France, showing visual relationships between tomb and shrine

7   Deerhurst showing location of 'secret' chapels

8   Anglo-Saxon church, Corhampton

9   St Mary's Stoke d'Abernon. Visual relationships between north aisle (c.1190) and chancel (c.1250)

10   Wharram Percy church, showing the remains of the former Norman arcade in the south wall and the remains of the south aisle in the foreground

11   Doom painting, North Leigh church

12   Monastic ruins, Byland

13   Etching of Salisbury Cathedral in the eighteenth century by Jacob Schnebbelie showing former Hungerford and Beauchamp chapels at east end

14   Etching of Salisbury Cathedral in the eighteenth century by Jacob Schnebbelie detailing interior view of Beauchamp chapel

15   The Draper chantry chapel, Christchurch Priory

16   Langton chapel, Winchester Cathedral

17   Vaughan chapel, St David's Cathedral

18   Audley chapel, Salisbury Cathedral

19 'Stone-cage' chantry chapel of Bishop William Wykeham, Winchester Cathedral

20 Chantry-tomb of Giles de Bridport, Salisbury Cathedral

21 Ramryge chapel, St Albans Abbey

22 Chantry chapel of Henry V, Westminster Abbey (Courtesy of Dean and Chapter of Westminster Abbey)

23 Gower chantry chapel in nave screen, St David's Cathedral

24 Collegiate chapel Boyton (looking east)

25 Eton College chapel viewed from Windsor Castle

26 Thurbern chapel and court, Winchester College

27 Fromond chapel, Winchester College

28 Almshouses, Ewelme

29 Bridge chapel, Wakefield

30 Chantry chapel of St James over the medieval west gate, Warwick

31 Meyring chapel, Newark church

32 Depiction of 'Dance of Death' on panel of Markham chapel, Newark

33 Medieval reredos marking former location of chantry chapel at Chipping Norton church

34 Spourne chapel, Lavenham church

35 Old Basing church showing north and south chancel chapels

36 The Lane aisle, Cullompton church

37 Wooden pews, St Mary's Warwick

38 Plan of east end of Long Melford parish church showing location of Clopton chapels

39 Commemoration script to John Lane, Cullompton church

40 Detail of external decoration of Greenway chapel, Tiverton, showing ships and maritime symbols of founder's trade

41 Transept chapel, Crewkerne, looking south-west

42 Architectural detail on the Beauchamp chapel, Bromham

43 Depictions of saints on internal 'buttresses' of Lane aisle arcade, Cullompton

44 Carved panel featuring the Day of Judgment on the Babington memorial, Kingston-on-Soar church

45 Painted monograms, St John's chapel, Ewelme

46 Plan of east end of Winchester Cathedral showing location of chantry chapels, altars and shrine

47 Chantry chapel of Humphrey of Gloucester and site of St Alban's shrine, St Albans Abbey

48 Chantry chapel of Henry V and site of Edward the Confessor's shrine (Courtesy of Dean and Chapter of Westminster Abbey)

49 Fleming chapel, Lincoln Cathedral

50 Plan of east end of Lincoln Cathedral

51 Plan of east end of Tewkesbury Abbey

52 Chantry chapels and high altar, Tewkesbury Abbey

53 Tropenell chapel, Corsham church

54 Plan of east end of St John's, Winchester

55 Plan of Gower chantry chapel and other altars, Southwark Cathedral (drawn by author, from Hines, Cohen and Roffey 2004)

56 Asthall church showing the view to the chapel altar from the north aisle

57 Wadham chapel, Ilminster church, showing location of former altars

58 Chapels in the south greater transept, Lincoln Cathedral. Here the fore-shortened screens defined individual space but allowed for visual accessibility between respective altars. Furthermore, the now blocked doorway through to the aisle would have once provided a view to an altar in the nave screen

59 South Leigh church showing elevation squints or 'peep holes' inserted into the chapel screen. Note prayer desk by right-hand squint

60 The twelfth-century squint at Compton church, among one of the earliest in the country

61 Squint in the east wall of the Berkeley chapel, Christchurch Priory

62 Squints in east wall of Markham chapel, Newark church

63 Passage squint, Sherston church

64 Squints in east wall of de la Warr chapel, Boxgrove Priory

65 Plan of de la Warr chapel, Boxgrove Priory, showing visual relationships between chapel, Lady Chapel and high altar

66 Squint through to nave screen chapel from south aisle and transept, Lincoln Cathedral

67 Plan of south transept and nave at Lincoln Cathedral showing conjectured visual relationships between chapel altars

68 Reconstructed visual relationships between chapels/high altar at St David's Cathedral

69 St David's Cathedral. High altar squint looking east

70 St David's Cathedral. High altar squint looking west from Vaughan chapel

71 Conjectured visual relationships between chapel altars/high altar at Cirencester churchl

72 Reconstructed view-sheds between chapels and high altar at Holy Trinity, Bradford-on-Avon

73 Plan of north chapel at Brympton d'Evercy church showing cluster of memorials slabs and tombs

74 Tomb altar in Wadham chapel, Ilminster church

75   Ewelme church. Effigy monument of Alice, Duchess of Suffolk, with a view through to south chapel

76   Despenser chantry chapel and effigy at Tewkesbury Abbey

77   Early sixteenth-century Easter sepulchre and tomb of John Waller, Stoke Charity church

78   Transi-tomb of John Fitzalan and Lady Chapel squint

79   Reconstruction of the sight-line from the nave to the altar in the Gyvernay chapel, Limington church indicating how the tomb obstructed the former sight-line into the chapel

80   Former decorated tomb recess, Stafford chapel, North Bradley

81   Blocked arch to former south chantry chapel, St Michael's, Southampton

82   Medieval screen reused as a post-Reformation pew, Gaddesby church

83   Internal view of Norreys' chapel, Rycote

84   Oddington church showing post-Reformation painting including Royal coat of arms over chancel arch, and biblical texts in chancel niches

85   Arrangement of Hungerford tombs, Farleigh Hungerford

86   Post-Reformation tombs, south chapel, Old Basing

87   Ludgershall church. Brydges tomb and chapel, seen from the nave

88   The chancel of Asthall church showing nineteenth-century wall paintings

89   The former chantry priest's house, Frome, now an electrical appliance shop

COLOUR PLATES

1   Wharram Percy church

2   Medieval painting of the 'Doom', or Day of Judgment, South Leigh church

3   The Harys chapel (*c.*1520), Christchurch Priory

4   Chantry chapel of Bishop Fox (1500-28), Winchester Cathedral

5   Chantry chapel of Bishop Gardiner (1531-55), Winchester Cathedral

6   St George's chapel, Windsor

7   Fifteenth-century Beauchamp chapel, St Mary's, Warwick

8   Fitzalan chapel and tomb of Thomas and Beatrix Fitzalan (*c.*1415), Arundel

9   Henry VII chapel, Westminster Abbey (Dean and Chapter of Westminster Abbey)

10   Bridge chapel, Wakefield

11   Markham chapel (*c.*1505), Newark church

12 Spring chapel (*c.*1525), Lavenham church
13 South wall of Clopton chapel, Long Melford, showing decorative panels, niches and painted inscriptions (*c.*1490s)
14 Greenway chantry chapel, Tiverton church (*c.*1517)
15 Elaborately decorated east gable of Beauchamp chapel, Devizes. Note large central niche once holding an image of the Virgin Mary
16 Elaborate western façade of the fourteenth-century chapel at Gaddesby church
17 Sixteenth-century Babington monument and chantry chapel as seen from the chancel at Kingston-on-Soar parish church
18 Fan vault, Wilcote chantry chapel, North Leigh (*c.*1440)
19 Interior of St John's chapel, Ewelme
20 Sixteenth-century Christ on the Lily Cross and rebus for John Leigh ('le Leigh' or 'Leigh Leigh') in Leigh chapel, Godshill
21 Detail of Lydgate's verses, Clopton chantry chapel, Long Melford church
22 Chantries of Bishop Beaufort (1405-1447) and Wayneflete (1447-86) crowd around the former site of St Swithun's shrine, Winchester Cathedral
23 The chantry chapel of Margaret Countess of Salisbury (d.1541) last direct descendant of the Plantagenets, next to the high altar, Christchurch Priory
24 De la Warr chantry chapel, Boxgrove Priory
25 'Enraptured in timeless adoration'. Detail of gilt-bronze effigy of Richard Beauchamp (d.1439), St Mary's, Warwick
26 Tomb of Lady Eleanor Percy (*c.* 1365), Beverley Minster
27 Fourteenth-century Easter sepulchre and tomb, Lincoln Cathedral
28 Chantry chapel and transi-tomb of Bishop Fleming (*c.*1425), Lincoln Cathedral
29 Post-Reformation pews in the former chantry chapel, Rycote

KEY TO PLANS:

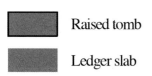

Raised tomb

Ledger slab

Altar/position of priest

ACKNOWLEDGEMENTS

I would like to thank Professor Michael Hicks and Professor Barbara Yorke for reading and commenting on early drafts of chapters, as well the staff and students of the University of Winchester, who have helped me explore some of the themes of this research in meetings, conversation, lectures and seminars. Others who have previously read and commented on various aspects of this work include Dr Clive Burgess, Professor Roberta Gilchrist, Dr Pam Graves, Professor Tom James, Dr Beat Kumin and Dr Andrew Reynolds. However, any inaccuracies are mine. I am also indebted to the University of Winchester for funding much of this project. Thank you also to Myra Wilkinson for copy-editing and compiling the index and to my brother Steven for computer support. I would also like to thank my wife, Suna, for her support during this busy time.

AUTHOR'S NOTE:
All date ranges in the text are for periods of incumbency/reign unless otherwise stated.

CHAPTER 1

INTRODUCTION

The subject of medieval chantry chapels is one that until recently has been largely neglected by archaeologists. Consequently the study of such complex monuments has primarily been within the remit of historians and art historians. Although of much value, the limitations of such defined approaches has meant that whilst we know much about their forms, architecture and patronage, we know very little about how chantries performed in practice, their relationship to the rest of church space and importantly, the wider social dimension behind their foundation. The majority of former chantry chapels are now lost to us. During the periods of reformation many where dismantled or destroyed, or converted to other uses. However, some still remain in part to offer a unique insight into the former nature of these foundations. These structures, although much altered with time, are still a noticeable feature of many parish churches and cathedrals. This book does not intend to be an exhaustive or comprehensive survey of such examples and it will not dwell on architectural detail unless it informs on religious experience. Rather it adopts a thematic approach, synthesising archaeological approaches with relevant documentary sources and discussing aspects of chantry chapel foundation, design and spatial arrangements with reference to some of the best surviving examples. Overall it discusses how such monuments were devised as medieval strategies for the afterlife – mechanisms by which the welfare of one's soul could, in theory, be assured. Furthermore, it will consider the wider impact that chantry chapels had on medieval church space and discuss how many chapels were important components in an increasingly complex ritual landscape. It will also examine the long view of the evolution of chantry chapels, considering the emergence of purgatorial doctrine in the Anglo-Saxon period and its influence on the churches and monasteries of the period.

In essence, a chantry was a foundation and endowment of a mass by one or more benefactors, to be celebrated at an altar, for the souls of the founders and other specified persons. The religious basis for the foundation of a chantry concerned medieval beliefs in the afterlife, specifically the idea of purgatory, which by the late medieval period had come to dominate both the world view of the ordinary people and the consequent religious practices both countenanced and proliferated by the church. Thus chantries were a direct strategy for the medieval afterlife and a mechanism to benefit souls in purgatory. Throughout the medieval period, purgatory was viewed as a penitential state where the sinful soul was purged of its venal sins and therefore able to reach Heaven and eventual salvation. It was a place, or a state, where the soul, shorn of its impermanent and corrupting corporeal form, was purged of the sin of past misdeeds. Purgatory, to the medieval mind, occupied a very real location in both time and space. However, there seems to have been some confusion, or lack of agreement at least, on what the exact nature of purgatory actually was. To some, it represented an antechamber to Heaven; a place of trial, but a place in which eventual salvation was assured. To others, however, purgatory represented a very real state of ordeal and suffering which could last almost for an eternity. Consequently, the way one acted in life informed and had direct consequences on the amount of time one spent in purgatory. Barring a life of extraordinary saintliness, however, most medieval people anticipated a stay of some length in purgatory. The most a person could hope for was a speedy deliverance. The fact that time spent in purgatory could be quantified meant that certain mechanisms could, in theory, be devised to intercede in the process. For this the dead had to rely on the living and often on certain related contingencies set up in life, such as chantry foundation. These intercessory strategies presumed that certain positive and directed activities or actions carried out by the living, such as dedicated masses and prayers, had some influence upon the dead. The role of saints as intercessors was often implicit in chantry foundation and the petitioning of saints through prayers and devotional practice was viewed as being particularly efficacious. The intercession of saints can be practically demonstrated at South Leigh parish church, for example. Here the south wall of the nave exhibits a fifteenth-century painting of St Michael weighing a soul. To his right, the Virgin Mary can be seen discreetly tipping the scales with her hand in the supplicant's favour (*1*).

Technically, a 'chantry' was a service rather than a physical entity and hence not visible archaeologically. The majority of chantries were of a temporary

1 Medieval wall painting, South Leigh, depicting St Michael and the Virgin Mary 'tipping the scales'

duration only and generated very little in the way of physical remains, as they were simply celebrated at existing altars. However, a number of chantries, founded usually by wealthier men and women, but also by collectives such as guilds and fraternities, were intended to last in perpetuity. These perpetual chantries were often in the form of dedicated chapels that appropriated or added to existing church space (*2*). Many of these endowments were provided with a physical context in the shape of altars, tombs, fixtures and fittings, and designated areas or structures such as chapels. These dedicated places could take the form of attached structures or side-chapels and areas of church space sealed off or defined by screens. It is this context for chantry foundation that usually provides the surviving, often fragmentary physical evidence and forms the basis for this book.

2 Early sixteenth-
century Lamb
chapel, Devizes

A STRATEGY FOR THE MEDIEVAL AFTERLIFE

The first documented chantry chapels emerged in the mid-thirteenth century. From this period until the Reformation of the sixteenth century, they were often outstanding additions to church space, introducing new forms of architectural innovation and display as well as new and varied liturgies. In some cases chantry chapels outclassed their churches architecturally and in many instances they provided a much needed addition to church fabric, particularly in the parish churches. Importantly, they also introduced supplementary priests and in some examples, such as medieval hospitals, chantry foundation was an important source of income, enabling these institutions to function effectively. Perpetual chantries were often funded by grants of land or property, which enabled a regular source of income to be provided and made sure that the chantry had sufficient income to survive in the ensuing centuries after the death of the founder, although some chantries, through bad management, appropriation or economic problems, did not last their full term.

However, the role of the chantry was not just limited to the performance of masses for the dead; such masses were also a key component of religious experience for the living. The mass was the central element of medieval religion and the foundation and endowment of chantries provided extra and often more varied masses in a period when divine service was particularly popular.

CHANTRIES AND LATE MEDIEVAL RELIGIOUS PRACTICE: VISION AND MEMORY

The importance of the mass in late medieval popular religion was paramount; as well as being the central Christian rite, its performance was also seen in the context of intercession as a unit of cumulative merit – the more masses said, the less time spent in purgatory. Chantries were therefore a specific response to the development of purgatorial beliefs, particularly from the thirteenth century onwards, and the belief that the mass was a unit of intercessory value. Medieval society was a largely illiterate one, with the exception of many of the clergy. The main medium, therefore, for the communication of religious experience was through the visual senses. Some of the emphasis was on direct visual communion with the host at the point of elevation during the mass, discussed in detail later, but there was also more indirect visual contact with the host through the architectural elements of churches and chantry chapels themselves, for example in the images, paintings and memorials. Most late medieval churches, to varying extents, were lavishly decorated. The use of embroidered altar cloths, hangings and veils, sculpture, painting, colours and light played an important part in creating a symbolic world, a 'vision of Heaven', that is attested to by surviving accounts and inventories, as well as fragmentary physical evidence. The celebration of the mass was the central point around which this vision revolved. In the larger churches and monasteries, the mass was often celebrated at different periods throughout the day at specific altars. It was, of course, also a key element of the most important festival and holiday in the Christian calendar, Easter Week. Through the performance of the mass, ultimate proof was provided that Christ had died and that souls could be saved by his sacrifice.

An essential component of the mass was the Elevation of the Host when the Eucharist, to the believer, was quite literally transubstantiated into the living flesh of Christ and held aloft by the celebrating priest for the observing laity to witness. During the mass, particularly privately endowed masses, or 'chantries', the prayers of the community were particularly valued – the more prayers, it was believed, the more powerfully enhanced the intercessory element of the ritual. The laity, in turn, benefited from even more elaborate and plentiful ceremonies and the spiritual efficacy of the mass itself. It also sustained an inherent feeling of spiritual and psychological security from it. Consequently, according to historian John Bossy, there was something for everyone in observing the Elevation of the Host, for the mystically inclined, the irretrievably mundane, the devout individualist and the communal fanatic. Transubstantiation itself offered not only the potential of salvation, but also the very act itself of the bread turning to flesh offered a very personal message of transformation. One could aspire to change. To the medieval religious, the mass therefore offered a message both inspirational and relevant to all, and one that, importantly, relied upon visual participation.

The physical structure and decoration of the medieval church was partly devised to induce a mood of reverence, to refine or sharpen the senses and to engage the emotions with the spiritual truth that was both stated and enacted. It was to provide a veritable vision of Heaven. Crucially, the space of many late medieval churches, and to an extent monastic churches, was ordered to emphasise the importance of the mass in religious practice. Space was often devised to provide optimal visual communion with the high altar and between the high altar and the various other altars which, on particular occasions, were also celebrating mass. Tombs and memorials and familial and heraldic devices were deliberately positioned to 'intrude' on the rituals, often juxtaposed with other forms of religious imagery. Their location was highly visible and forged an all-important visual association with the mass being celebrated. In a sense, they inevitably imposed their memory on the viewer. Archaeologist Pamela Graves calls the use of such methods and devices 'presencing mechanisms' and suggests they are a 'powerful technology for salvation'. To the medieval mind, the association of the individual with the ritual of the mass acted as an *aide-mémoire* and as such was an indirect and mnemonic petition for prayer. However, this relationship was not purely one-way, as the spiritual benefits of the mass, the increase in divine service afforded by individually founded chantry altars and the introduction of new and varied forms of devotional practice were beneficial to the whole community. They contributed to a varied and colourful religious experience. Furthermore, the associated embellishment and sometimes expansion of church space and fabric afforded by personal endowments and related gifts, also indicate that the relationship was mutually beneficial.

The foundations of chantries therefore offered short-term, long-term and perpetual strategies for the afterlife. As such they were an important component of a wider set of practices designed to engage intercession and evoke memory over time.

SHORT-TERM AND LONG-TERM STRATEGIES FOR THE AFTERLIFE

Throughout the late medieval period, the church offered two main types of intercession for souls in purgatory. These can generally be described as short-term and long-term strategies. In practical terms, both types began with the death of the individual and rites carried out at the place of death. The funeral of the deceased and the celebration of the Placebo, Dirige and Requiem frequently marked the beginning of an often perpetual ritual journey. Some funerals were ostentatious affairs and the spectacle provided by the rituals as well as the giving of gifts helped to impose the memory of the deceased more firmly on the minds of the people. The will of Joanne Hungerford in 1411 provides us with an insight into the level of detail behind the organisation of such events:

> ... I desire on my burial day that twelve torches and two tapers burn about my body and that twelve poor women holding the said torches be clothed in russet with linen hoods and having stockings and shoes suitable ... also clothing for sons and daughters and sons and daughters of domestic servants ...

Short-term strategies were generally represented by a period of intensive memorial practice, such as the celebration of the 'Trental', or 30 masses, to be said over the ensuing month. The Trental was relatively inexpensive and therefore popular. However, for the wealthiest (or the more sinful?) requests for masses in the hundreds or even thousands were not unusual. For example, John Clopton of Long Melford paid for 2000 masses to be celebrated within a month after his death, whilst the will of Joanne Hungerford requested that 'all possible speed after my decease my executors cause three thousand masses to be said for my soul and for the souls of all the faithful deceased'. This period of intensive intercessory activity was seen to be particularly efficacious and was sometimes referred to as the 'months mind' (interestingly, it has parallels in other religions such the traditional period of intercessory practice outlined in the Tibetan Buddhist *Bardo Thodol*). The cultural historian Philippe Ariès has suggested that medieval funerary rituals evoked a bout of temporarily heightened remembrance. However, Ariès notes, memory eventually subsided as the body of the deceased decayed and disappeared. Although this may be true for the majority of cases, for wealthier individuals the perpetuation of memory could be physically inscribed in the form of a well-placed and visually impressive tomb, dedicated work of art or the foundation of a chantry chapel, and the structured performance of perpetual memorial liturgy. Such devices helped reinforce the memory of the individual within the context of the church and its shared rituals. In a sense, individual memory became a component of the church fabric as well as on occasion, in the case of chantries, communal religious practice.

At their most basic, long-term strategies were also represented by obits or anniversary celebrations, where the name of the deceased was spoken or read out. In most cases these were celebrated once a year at a specified date (not always the date of death). In some instances, the anniversary involved an exact replication of the funeral prayers and masses held in the church at the original funeral. At the other end of the scale of long-term strategies was the foundation and endowment of perpetual chantries, sometimes housed in their own chapel or, for the wealthiest donors, collegiate chapels.

An important aspect of these latter strategies was their relationship to communal long-term memory. Over the last 30 years, psychologists have recognised two types of long-term memory: episodic memory and semantic memory. Episodic memory concerns information specific to a particular context, such as a time and place, while semantic memory is a structured record of facts, concepts and skills that have been acquired over time. In these terms we can perhaps understand how the location of tombs and memorials, the design of chantry chapels and the perpetual performance of associated dedicated masses acted to provide a context for repeated exposure of the deceased to individual memory. In effect, they evoked a continual stimulus or the rehearsal of a piece of information that gradually worked its way into communal long-term memory.

The medieval chantry was one of the most important and influential religious institutions within the late medieval period. It was a key component of religious practice in the monasteries and the parishes and, as well as providing monuments dedicated to private piety and individual memorial practice, it was of some significance to the wider society. Before moving on to examine the origins of the medieval chantry chapel, we will set this study in a broader context by providing an overview of previous work, traditional perspectives and the various sources and approaches that can be applied to the study of medieval chantry chapels.

CHAPTER 2

PERSPECTIVES ON THE STUDY
OF MEDIEVAL CHANTRY CHAPELS

TRADITIONAL AND HISTORICAL PERSPECTIVES ON THE MEDIEVAL CHANTRY

The majority of studies concerning medieval chantries have largely been from a documentary-based or art historical perspective. The monuments themselves have received comparatively little archaeological attention when compared with the study of monastic or parish churches overall, and little in the way of detailed survey has been carried out. Much of the deficit lies with the smaller parish examples – the more architecturally impressive examples were founded in the more prominent institutions and consequently chantry chapels founded in the greater monastic houses and cathedrals have received more academic attention. The work of Geoffrey Cook, in particular, provides an excellent, if now outdated, survey of some of the more outstanding examples, drawn largely from former monasteries and cathedrals. In addition, Cook has written a general survey of collegiate foundations. Much work has also been carried out on the better known and individual collegiate foundations such as the study of St George's in Windsor, edited by Colin Richmond and Eileen Scarff and at the other end of the scale, the study by John Goodall of Ewelme, Oxfordshire. The intercessory functions of medieval guilds have been considered nationally by Herbert Westlake and regionally by Virginia Bainbridge (Cambridgeshire), David Crouch (Yorkshire) and Ken Farnhill (East Anglia) among others.

In the context of parish church chantry foundations – many of which are not recognisably intact – Kathleen Wood-Legh has written the most comprehensive historical study to date. She considers the wider social and economic, as well as religious, role of the medieval parish chantry, albeit with little emphasis on the physical evidence from surviving examples. Such historical emphasis on the parish church chantry also involved more focused studies of localised chantry foundations but, as Michael Hicks has stated, much of this historical research has been directed towards specific status groups and particular classes of record. Consequently he suggests that without some understanding of the institutions themselves, breakdowns of benefactors and types of benefactor are of little use. In effect, they tell us little about the practical role of such monuments. However, studies carried out by the historian Clive Burgess, focusing in particular on the parish churches in London and Bristol, has highlighted the wide impact and effect that such foundations had, not just on memorial and private piety, but on the wider community and parish as a whole. In particular he has shown the important contribution that surviving churchwardens' accounts can provide for the study of chantries and related lay piety.

Despite the insights that documentary and architectural study can provide with regard to the popularity of religion prior to the Reformation, archaeological examination of church fabric can illustrate further aspects of religious practice which may only be hinted at in historical documents. Here, the combination of relevant historical sources, such as accounts and wills, can be used in conjunction with the detailed archaeological analysis of surviving church fabric. For example, in a comparative study of Devon and Norfolk, Pamela Graves has produced an alternative to generalised and traditional studies of late medieval religion by combining the evidence presented by historical accounts, such as wills, with the surviving fabric of medieval churches. In this sense, she moves beyond the often standardised and limited documents themselves to investigate the actual physical imprints of the past and how testators left their presence within the fabric of their churches. However, it must be said that the survival of documents, particularly those relating to smaller, often rural parish churches or monastic houses, is rare. In the case of chantry foundations, in many instances there are no surviving records. Here archaeology must necessarily lead the way. Jonathan Finch, in his study of commemoration and church monuments in Norfolk, indicates how much the systematic study of the surviving church fabric can reveal about the form and function of religious belief in relation to memorial practice. More recently, the present author has illustrated how the spatial and structural analysis of parish chantry chapels, with particular reference to examples drawn from the south and west of England, can shed light on how such monuments worked in practice. However, it should be borne in mind that, like the documents themselves, distinct physical evidence of religious practice and devotion as presented by the fabric of medieval churches is relatively rare. Most religious houses, except for the greater cathedrals, have now disappeared and those that survive have been drastically restructured. Most parish churches have been reordered and 'restored' in the centuries following the Reformation; their former religiously-inspired decorative elements and fixtures and fittings are lost to us. Nevertheless, detailed archaeological investigation can reconstruct many aspects of chantry foundation that may still survive hidden away in the extant fabric. Furthermore, a detailed archaeological examination of surviving examples can help to explain the various physical forms and components of chantry chapels and how they actually 'worked' in practice. Crucially it can shed light on elements of chantry foundation often neglected by traditional history-based approaches – that of the wider social role of chantry foundation in monastic and particularly parish churches, and considerations given over to the location and spatial aspects of their construction.

Before we examine the various types of chantry foundation in more detail we will first examine the methodological framework which assists their study and consider the various sources and approaches that can be applied to them.

SOURCES AND APPROACHES

Documentary Sources

Surviving documents can be a useful source of background information for the structural investigation of former chantries and chapels, as well as being able to provide circumstantial information regarding founders and foundation dates, location and dedication, for example. A range of primary documentary sources survives, in part, to provide potential information about chapel and chantry foundations and their goods. Of particular importance are the documents relating to the Statutes of Mortmain from 1279, a piece of legislation that declared that all chantry foundations must have a royal licence. The Statutes of Mortmain were introduced to prevent land continuing to fall into the 'dead hand' of the church, yet over 2000 licences were issued between the late thirteenth century and 1547. However, one should be aware that the amount of licences issued almost certainly exceeds the actual foundations themselves, as for one reason or another the actual endowment of the chantries may never have happened. Licences could also be ignored or evaded by legal means. However, such documents are of limited use; whilst identifying some endowments, they lack sufficient detail regarding the foundations themselves. They can therefore tell us very little about how chantries worked in practice and their various fixtures, fittings and internal arrangements.

For parish churches, churchwardens' accounts can provide insight into the internal fixtures, fittings and goods associated with chantry foundation. For example, Clive Burgess and Katherine French have demonstrated that these accounts can be a particularly fruitful source of information, as they address lay priorities, the community concerns behind chantry foundation and intercessory endowments. Unfortunately, the survival of such accounts is sporadic – for example less than 10 per cent of medieval accounts survives for the medieval diocese of Winchester, a diocese that encompassed much of southern England.

Medieval wills can also provide a useful source of background information. However, these are more problematical in that, as the historian Barrie Dobson points out, they frequently emerge as declarations of intent rather than evidence of creation. Wills are also limited as they are often too specific and provide lists of gifts and grants but do not tell us about long-term religious involvement. Nevertheless they can provide some useful details about particular burial arrangements in chapels and the details behind their endowment.

Many important documentary sources relate to surveys of monuments carried out during the Reformation. One of the most important of these was the *Valor Ecclesiasticus*, a survey and evaluation of every religious house prior to its dissolution. The documents that relate directly to the dissolution of the chantries in the mid-sixteenth century (the so-called chantry certificates) can identify individual chantry foundations and often their goods, services and location within the church. It is important to remember, however, that they only provide information about chantries surviving in 1547. Neither the certificates nor the *Valor* generally contain information about those chantries founded in monasteries and parish churches that had already been dissolved or had declined prior to the sixteenth century. It is also possible that certain chantries were overlooked or concealed and therefore did not feature in these surveys. For the greater religious houses of the medieval period, surviving documentary records are more frequent. These can take the form of bishops' registers and visitation records, calendars of obits and documents relating to individual chantry foundations including cartularies, rentals and lists of priests. These documents normally focus specifically on income and expenditure and tell us little about the form, location and internal arrangements of individual chapels.

Archaeological Approaches

Traditionalist approaches within late medieval archaeology have placed primary emphasis on descriptive interpretations of the archaeological record. In the case of medieval churches and chapels, for example, whether standing or excavated, various interpretations might include the physical layout, details of building materials and the recovery of phase plans. These interpretations are largely within a historical framework, and therefore rather limited and narrow in their potential scope. Moreover, studies of the medieval church have often been over-reliant on documentary sources. This is partly to do with the fact that much of the available literature on medieval archaeology has served to illustrate the medieval past in purely historic, document-derived terms. Hence, at face value, many historical documents relating to chantry foundation suggests that they were primarily private institutions. This is not helped by the cursory examination of some of the better surviving and grander cathedral examples, which, with their appropriation of church space and personal display of elitist symbols, would support their interpretation as wholly individual and selfish monuments. However, a contextualised approach to such monuments, embracing a wider set of sources, can present a different picture in many cases. In particular, certain theoretical approaches, drawn largely from social and anthropological studies and often formerly applied to prehistoric sites, can provide an investigative framework in which to examine chantry chapels. Such approaches can address how factors such as the requirements of the liturgy and the ambitions and concerns of the patrons affected the space and fabric of the medieval church. For too long now, church archaeology has concentrated on the obvious aspects of the material record. Emphasis on establishing phase plans within a historical framework has overshadowed explanations as to why these changes might have occurred and how they related to types of religious practice and experience, as well as to social relationships. It is one of the roles of archaeological theory to redress this imbalance.

Furthermore, one of the problems, traditionally, with the architectural study of standing buildings is that examination can sometimes be unfocused and lacking in objectivity. The archaeological examination of church fabric can provide an objective account of the evidence available and a form of evidence that may go beyond the documentary sources. In particular, the analysis of church space can provide an insight into how religion was experienced within the churches. In the case of chantry chapels, this includes the analysis of chapel space and internal arrangements, location and the examination of spatial relationships between associated features such as altars, shrines and tombs. In the case of monasteries it may also help to investigate the location of chapels in relationship to pilgrim ambulatories, saints' shrines and clerical processional routes. As previously noted, visual relationships are particularly significant with regard to the visibility of ritual foci, religious images and, importantly, the performance of the mass. Here such applications may help investigate aspects of visibility: sight-lines and associated spatial ordering.

View-shed analysis, or the examination of lines of sight, has been previously applied mainly to prehistoric landscape contexts, but it is equally applicable to the study of monuments such as churches and chantry chapels. This approach is invaluable in reconstructing the spatial relationship between chapels and chantries and the church and community. It assists our understanding of why monuments are placed in particular areas of chapel topography. It indicates the importance of public visual access to the symbols, images and features of chapel space and fabric, as well as the nature and level of visual participation in the rituals enacted within them, particularly with regard to the mass. Visual relationships in chapel and church topography can be examined by reconstructing sight-lines, or view-sheds, the basis of which lies in the application of what is termed a 'phenomenological' approach – again an approach normally confined to landscapes – to surviving church space and fabric. This approach consists of examining specific areas of the church and their internal arrangements, and establishing what could have been seen from certain areas and how features or structural elements such as tombs, squints, walls and windows, for example, may have supported, inhibited or obstructed former sight-lines. This approach is designed to answer particular questions, such as whether it was important for chapel altars to be viewed from public areas of the church, or if subsidiary altars had a clear view of the high altar. It may also reveal to what extent personal and religious symbols, tombs and monuments were deliberately located to place them in public or clerical lines of sight, and what this can reveal about the importance of vision within medieval ritual. Ultimately, the analysis of church space should be coupled with an examination of church fabric. Thus, structural changes and additions and the placement of windows and screens to emphasise formerly important ritual areas may shed light on the forms of religious experience enacted in these places.

Spatial information collected from chapels can also cast light on the level of personal and collective participation in intercessory practice. As Eamon Duffy has noted, one of the key issues in the study of the late medieval church is to what extent chantries enforced a privatisation of lay religious experience. With regards to this the main question is: to what extent were chantry chapels wholly 'private' enclaves? Spatial analysis of many chantry chapels and their settings suggests that such monuments reflected a 'personalisation' rather than a privatisation of church space. Therefore, chantry chapels, particularly in the parishes, were public monuments: they nourished everyone's religious experience and cannot be seen as a symptom of mere exclusivity. Former lines of sight can be reconstructed and viewed in the context of the development of collectively accessible spatial geographies. As will be seen, vision was the most important medium for religious experience. Therefore the analysis of lines of sight and visual relationships is crucial – one might say indispensable – to our understanding of medieval religious practice. It may be able to tell us whether chantry masses were visible or invisible from the body of the church, particularly the more publicly accessible areas such as the nave and aisles, or only from within the chapels themselves. The reconstruction of visual relationships also takes into account the association between personal and religious images, the use of light and the consequent location of windows, and the positioning of monuments to place them within the line of vision or obstruct it. Importantly, such reconstruction can also provide an insight into how chapel space was reorganised over time, particularly with regard to the Reformation which, as will be seen, brought about the drastic and conscious reorganisation of former ritual space.

Many important history-based studies of the chantry regard its origins as largely a thirteenth-century phenomenon, as it is in this period that formal documents relating to the foundation of a 'chantry' – from the Latin *cantaria*, 'to sing' – begin to appear. However, although the term 'chantry' certainly dates to the late medieval period, the actual concept of the chantry as a personalised strategy for the afterlife was a much earlier feature of religious life. Indeed, notions of an afterlife containing a penitential or purgatorial dimension had been around since the Anglo-Saxon period. We shall now examine the archaeological evidence for early related memorial practice and consider how individual strategies for the afterlife may have been constructed in the centuries prior to the first official chantry foundations.

CHAPTER 3

THE AFTERLIFE AND
THE ANGLO-SAXON CHURCH:
THE FOUNDATIONS OF
MEMORIAL PRACTICE

Before we examine late medieval beliefs in the afterlife and the form and function of the later medieval chantry chapel we first need to consider the historical foundations from which they emerged. This chapter will therefore examine the evidence for memorial and intercessory practices prior to the first documented chantry chapels of the thirteenth century. It will not attempt to provide an exhaustive survey of what is a potentially complex subject in its own right, but will consider elements of early commemorative practice based on primarily archaeological evidence, elements that may have been influential to the later development of chantry chapels. It will thus provide a broad introduction and set a contextual background for later discussion, and it will work on the assumption that the later medieval chantry did not just 'materialise' in the thirteenth century, but evolved out of a set of earlier practices, both social and religious.

PRE–CHRISTIAN MEMORIAL PRACTICE IN ANGLO–SAXON ENGLAND

In the absence of documentary accounts and memorial architecture, the analysis of burial sites provides a unique window into contemporary beliefs concerning the afterlife in early Anglo-Saxon England. Archaeological evidence for Anglo-Saxon burial practice prior to the widespread Christian conversions of the seventh century reveals, in many cases, the preparation of the body for a perceived afterlife. The presence of grave goods from pagan cemeteries, such as the princely burials of Sutton Hoo, Suffolk, suggests that the body was equipped to confront an afterlife not too dissimilar from that of its natural life. Excavations in the 1930s of the seventh-century ship burial at Mound 1 Sutton Hoo brought to light a range of domestic and personal artefacts including objects associated with feasting, entertainment, costume and warfare. This burial and other furnished examples from the period such as the bed burial from Swallowcliffe Down, Wiltshire, suggest that the afterlife was perceived as having had some form of spatial, temporal and familiar element to it. Furthermore, for the living, the presence of what has been termed 'houses of the dead' – four-post structures around pagan cremation burials at Appledown, Sussex – have been suggested as possible evidence for the long-term veneration of the dead. Similarly, evidence for structures associated with early burials has been found at Bishopstone, Sussex, and Polhill, Kent. At Yeavering, Northumberland, a linear arrangement of sixth-century burials may have been aligned to a central timber post, possibly a totemic or memorial focus. The existence of an essentially pagan-derived memorial practice is implied in later Christian sources. A homily of Pope Leo IV (reigned 847-55) for example, admonishes the practice of *carmina diabolica* (literally 'diabolical song') at burials, and Ælfric, writing in the 990s, forbids the singing of heathen songs and funeral feasts.

The range of burial practices in the pagan Anglo-Saxon period was diverse and largely informal, and ranged from inhumations and cremations to secondary burials within prehistoric barrows, such as at Swallowcliffe, and former henge monuments, as at Yeavering. Such variation suggests that burial practices were influenced by local or tribal custom or even individual responses to the afterlife and that consequently no orthodox or prescribed universal belief system existed. The coming of Christianity in the final years of the sixth century may have offered a more formal set of practices rooted in historical tradition and supported by texts and a complex and no doubt dramatic liturgy. With this, it can be argued, came a more credible and perhaps convincing set of strategies for the afterlife. It is therefore possible that the Anglo-Saxons forsook their customary ideas of an afterlife, not unlike that on earth, in favour of Christian concepts of the afterlife and the surrounding belief that the church offered a set of valid and clearly defined strategies concerning it. Consequently Christianity offered a more efficient and universally applied means of intercession than previously available. This was especially attractive to an Anglo-Saxon elite, on whom the monasteries – powerhouses of conversion – ultimately relied. In turn, the wealthy Anglo-Saxon benefactors were provided with an active memorial, the fabric of which would resonate with the prayers and devotions of the pious for centuries to come. These institutions were therefore a statement of local prestige linked with intercessory and memorial concerns. Behind them was a belief that there was an intermediary 'penitential' state between this world and the next upon which the church had some level of influence. This was a crucial point, for here not only could short-term preparations be made with respect to the corporeal remains in the context of 'Christian burial', but longer-term strategies could be initiated for the soul in the afterworld. It would perhaps be a mistake to label this penitential state as 'purgatory' in the later medieval sense of the word, as this was a state that was as yet ill-defined. Over the following centuries, however, it was a concept that was continually evolving and that came to play a formative role in the development of the Anglo-Saxon church.

'PURGATORY' AND THE ANGLO-SAXON CHURCH

It was only in the twelfth and thirteenth centuries that the formal definition of purgatory as a 'penitential' afterlife, a state where sin would be expunged through metaphysical ordeal, was formally recognised by the church. During this period, doctrinal developments, particularly within the universities of Paris, established a formal means of dealing with the penances attached to purgatory. These doctrinal developments were largely ratified at the Council of Lyon in 1274. However, beliefs revolving around a notion of 'purgatory' as an intermediate and penitential world between Heaven and Hell can be traced much earlier. The French social historian Jacques le Goff has acknowledged that precedents can be identified in the apocryphal II Maccabees and the Classical teachings of the early Greek fathers Origen (third century) and Clement of Alexandria (d. *c*.215). Moreover, their teachings bear conceptual similarities with the earlier Jewish pseudographia of Enoch and with the Vedic Hindu 'three paths of the dead', which date to at least the sixth century BC. Moreover, as we have seen, notions of a 'purgatory' can perhaps also be seen in the afterlife 'journeys' of the pagan Anglo-Saxons.

A practical element that was crucial to medieval memorial practice was intercession; the ability to intercede on the soul's behalf. One essential means by which this was facilitated was through the active contribution of prayers for the dead. Here the living – and not just members of monastic communities but the laity also – could actively influence the welfare of the soul of the dead. One of the earliest documented accounts of prayers for an individual soul comes from the *Confessions* of the late fourth-century theologian St Augustine of Hippo. In this account, which contains prayers for his deceased mother, Augustine implores that

> ... all she wanted was that we should remember her at your altar ... for she knew that at your altar we receive the holy victim ... inspire those who read this book to remember Monica, your servant, at your altar.

The relevance of this excerpt is that it tells us three key things about early intercessory prayers. Firstly, Augustine's conviction that prayers can be influential; secondly, the relevance of the 'holy victim', or Eucharist; and finally that the participation of others is especially beneficial (significantly, it is these three factors that would form the core of later medieval chantry-based practice).

One of the more important figures in the formation of intercessory doctrine was Pope Gregory the Great (*c.*540-604). It has been claimed that Gregory was the first to erect an altar over the tomb of St Peter in Rome, thereby forging a link between Eucharistic worship and the veneration of relics. Gregory is also credited with introducing the 'Trental', a series of 30 intercessory masses which remained popular until the Reformation in the sixteenth century. In the tenth century the Trental appears as part of the memorial liturgy of the *Regularis Concordia*, composed at Winchester by the reforming Bishop Æthelwold. In the fifteenth century it occurs, for example, in the will of Edward Curteys of 1413, who requested 'Gregrestrental' to be celebrated after his death in the church of St Cuthbert, Wells.

Over 100 years after the death of Gregory, the eighth-century English monk Bede provided a more descriptive geography of the afterlife. In his *Homilies* he warns that some are taken after death by the flames of purgatorial fire and severely punished. Either they are cleansed of their vices by a long trial in this fire, or thanks to the prayers, alms, fasting, tears and Eucharistic offerings of their faithful friends they are delivered from punishment. In the *Vision of Drythelm*, Bede describes souls in purgatorial fire being helped by the offering of masses (*Historia Ecclesiastica* V: xii). In his account of the thegn Imma, Bede also attempted to introduce ideas about 'purgatory' and the efficacy of prayer. In this story, Imma is taken prisoner in a battle and kept in chains. His brother, who is a priest, thinks he is dead and collects a body he assumes to be Imma's, which he places in his church and over which he says special masses. The result is that Imma's physical, earthly chains fall off and it becomes impossible to bind him so that eventually he gains his freedom. Here, the message offers an analogy: if Imma had really been dead his brother would have 'released' him from limbo (*Historia Ecclesiastica* IV, 22). In the *Life of St Cuthbert*, Bede also refers to a petition for St Cuthbert to 'remember at mass my servant … who had died yesterday'. Like Gregory before him, Bede provides us with further insight into the nature of intercessory practice at this time that not only involved Eucharistic celebration, but also the consequence of good works through the giving of alms. These factors, which are highly significant and will be discussed in more detail later, indicate that purgatorial ideology and related intercessory practice was an important element of Anglo-Saxon religious belief at a relatively early date.

By the eleventh century, the so-called monastic revival in England had introduced a more formal and nationally-based codification of liturgical practice. At the heart of the monastic reforms lay the *Regularis Concordia* composed, as we saw earlier, at Winchester by Bishop Æthelwold in the 970s. The *Concordia* included prayers for the royal house, indicative perhaps of the growing popularity of personalised masses. This period also coincided with the development of formal rites associated with the consecration of cemeteries, including the use of prayers, masses and lights. Bequests of 'soul-scot', money set aside to provide prayers for the deceased, appear increasingly in Anglo-Saxon wills from the tenth century. For example, in her will of 950 the noblewoman Wynflaed bequeathed money to the monasteries of Shaftesbury and Wantage, as well as a personal grant to the nun Æthelflaed the White to be 'mindful of her soul'.

A few decades later, the *Liber Vitae*, produced at Hyde Abbey in Winchester in the 1030s, provided an actual visual representation of the afterlife, perhaps for the first time. Here, a triptych depicted the afterlife as divided into three places. At the top of the triptych, St Peter is shown welcoming the just into Heaven, while in the bottom panel, the damned are cast into the hell-mouth. However, between Heaven and Hell there is a third place, that of purgatory, where an angel, perhaps St Michael, can clearly be seen smiting a demon. Behind him, the souls of the dead are escorted away by angels. Not only does this depiction reveal to us this third realm between Heaven and Hell, but also the capacity of saints to intercede effectively on behalf of the soul. The role of saints as intercessors, or mediators, was a particularly important element of Christian memorial practice. The late seventh-century wooden coffin of St Cuthbert, for example, was inscribed with iconographic figures including Christ, the Apostles and the Virgin and Child. The particular choice of images and arrangements has been claimed by Chris Daniell and Victoria Thompson to be an 'embodiment of prayer literally embracing the corpse'. Thus, many early monasteries sought out and housed the relics of local saints. The early-medieval historian Barbara Yorke has made the observation that the popularity of local saints as intercessors may have had a secular precedence. In Anglo-Saxon society, local lords were often used to intercede with the king. Yorke suggests that people may have thought that Heaven worked in a similar way and that a local saint could intercede with God on their behalf. It is therefore no surprise that in the influential royal monastic foundations of Wessex in the ninth and tenth centuries, many of the local saints had familial links to the royal family.

A growing desire to provide some formal means of intercession for the dead was one of the main reasons for the relatively quick and widespread foundation of minsters (monastic houses) from the early seventh century onwards. Many of these early monasteries were established with the express intention that the founder's soul be 'remembered daily at the altar' and every form of benefaction carried with it an underlying obligation of personal intercession. These foundations, however, were inevitably the preserve of the elite and many of the early minsters were affiliated to a local lord. Institutionally, there was no set pattern to either the communal layout or the function of such early houses. Most minster communities consisted of around four or five monks, including one or two priests who were able to celebrate mass. Structurally, many of these early monastic houses conformed to a common layout of nave, chancel and, in many cases, lateral chambers or porticus, which were arranged much like later chapels and aisles. The function of the porticus has never been clearly defined and has therefore been subject to various interpretations, but it is likely that many of these structures provided a context for burial and related memorial practice.

THE PORTICUS: A CONTEXT FOR COMMEMORATION?

The porticus was an adjunct structure often attached to the north or south side of the church. It was a feature of many Anglo-Saxon churches such as the important early religious centres at Dover, Reculver and Winchester. Later foundations with porticus include St Laurence, Bradford-on-Avon and the minsters at Breamore (*3*), Deerhurst and Wareham. The function of the porticus has never been satisfactorily explained by architectural historians, having been variously described as 'liturgical envelopes' of the church, a place for tombs and relics, baptisteries and as monastic living quarters. Barbara Yorke has suggested that to the Anglo-Saxons it would appear that the term porticus was associated with elite burial in an ecclesiastical context and that some porticus, as at Canterbury, were physically part of churches, while some, it seems, could be free-standing burial structures, as Carolyn Heighway has argued for Gloucester. The label 'porticus' may also be misleading, as we assume from this that they were designed for an exclusive or specific function. Certainly we should distinguish between modern and historical applications of the term, since for some examples, such as Deerhurst, there is no direct contemporary record of its usage. We should also be aware that it is likely that the porticus may have served a variety of functions at particular times, as often did the chuches themselves.

It is possible that the porticus was an element of formal design adopted from continental models and that its function was largely dependent on local or individual concerns and priorities. However, the liminal position of the porticus, often flanking and open to the body of the church, might in many cases be suggestive of a specific primary religious and liturgical function. Archaeological and written evidence suggests that some early porticus were used as a place of burial. As such they offered an alternative to sanctions during the Anglo-Saxon period against burial within the church itself. Such structures brought the physical remains of the deceased into the spiritual sphere of the church without necessarily impinging directly on sacred space. At Saints Peter and Paul in Canterbury, the north porticus was used for the burial of the first English archbishops, whilst that to the south was for the royal family. The north side of the seventh-century monastic church at Jarrow was the funerary porticus for the founder, Benedict Biscop, and later abbots. Contemporary documents of the period recount that the head of King Edwin was buried in the porticus of St Gregory at York, whilst the rest of him, and also the body of King Oswiu, may have been buried in a similarly dedicated porticus at Whitby Abbey. The record of the burials of St Æthelflaed's indicate that she was buried in the eastern porticus at St Oswald's in Gloucester around 918. Excavations at the site conducted by Carolyn Heighway and Richard Bryant revealed the remains of a small structure abutting the east end of the church which they proposed as the burial place of Æthelflaed. At Buckfastleigh, excavations by Andrew Reynolds

3 Anglo-Saxon church, Breamore showing south-west porticus, later used as a porch and the south-east porticus attached to the tower

and Sam Turner uncovered the possible high-status burials of women within the north porticus of the pre-Conquest church. Evidence from this site also revealed the foundations of a possible screen dividing this area from the rest of the church and structural evidence suggests that the porticus was incorporated into the walls of the later south transept with its lateral chapel.

At Canterbury, the north porticus was dedicated to St Gregory and the southern one to St Martin. The existence of these dedications suggests the presence of altars, as technically it is the altar that is dedicated and not the structure. It is likely therefore that any masses performed at these altars had some relationship to the burials and were therefore of indirect intercessory merit. Excavations within the north porticus at Sherborne Abbey revealed evidence for a rectangular plaster platform which was suggested by the excavators to be part of the reliquary or tomb of St Wulfin. The porticus, it was claimed, may have been a place to accommodate distinguished laity. However it can also be suggested, on the basis of evidence for a saintly tomb and for a later fourteenth-century altar, that the porticus may have originally had a more liturgical or ritual purpose. In comparison, an early eleventh-century description of the church of St Riquer in France, written down about the same time as the porticus at Sherborne was constructed, informs us of the presence of a series of altars within 'transepts' and 'aisles'. The position of the internal doorways of the north and south porticus at St Oswald's in Gloucester (*4*) and at Deerhurst suggests a spatial emphasis on the east side of these structures. Likewise, the position of the doorway into the north porticus at St Laurence's, Bradford-on-Avon, could indicate the former location of an eastern altar or saint's shrine (*5*). The external doorway is deliberately positioned in the west end of the porticus north wall, which could indicate the provision for a liturgical space at the porticus's east end. The relationship between saintly relics and burial can be illustrated by the example of the late eighth-century church of St Apôtres, France. Here, a north chapel off the apse contained a single burial. A skewed east window in the chapel would have directed light upon an associated altar above or very close to the tomb, thereby acting as a form of spotlight. Furthermore, the position of this burial is noteworthy as it is directly related to the shrine of St Geneviève to the south within the apse. There is a direct visual relationship, or view-shed, between the two through the chapel arch to the shrine in the centre of the church choir (*6*). The implications behind visual relationships between monuments and other religious foci is pertinent and will be discussed in detail later, but is worth noting here.

The internal doorways of many porticus are narrow and may indicate an attempt to restrict access, particularly visual access, to the chamber. In effect, this created a degree of mysticism, an interplay between exposure and concealment for those looking within. Similarly, the position of the western

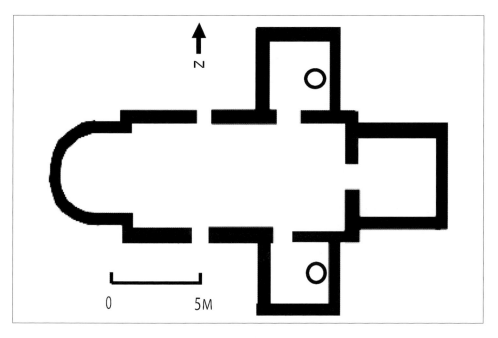

4 St Oswald's Gloucester, showing conjectured location of altars in porticus

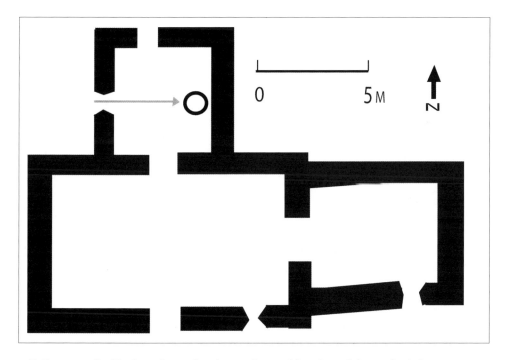

5 St Laurence, Bradford-on-Avon, showing conjectured location of altar and window highlighting the area

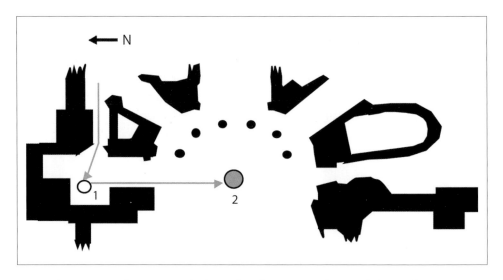

6 St Apôtres, France, showing visual relationships between tomb (1) and shrine (2)

window at Bradford-on-Avon – positioned so as to 'spotlight' the altar – also added to the overall effect. Furthermore, the location of some porticus, as adjuncts to the nave (an area traditionally assigned to lay pastoral activity) may indicate the social relationship between these spaces. This arrangement can be found at Bradford-on-Avon, Deerhurst, St Oswald's in Gloucester and Bishopstone in Sussex amongst others.

The French social historian Philippe Ariès has claimed that the ninth and tenth centuries witnessed a growing anxiety about death and the consequent need for stronger forms of personal intercession (Ariès, 1981). These, he further suggests, were the principal motives behind the major changes that took place in the structure of the mass at this period. It was also during this period that a closer connection was made between the idea of personal destiny and the use of penitential manuals, which outlined certain practices for the alleviation of personal sin during natural life. The evolution of penitential codes and manuals for evaluating sin marked a transition from collective to personal destiny and a change from passive commemoration to active memorial practice. The development and increasing popularity of formal intercessory doctrine may have been the drive behind the multiplication of subsidiary altars in churches, many of which could have served as a context for personal benefaction and memorial and intercessory masses. For example, on the continent, the early ninth-century monastic church at St Sauveur, France, had four altars and the idealised plan of the monastic church at St Gall, Switzerland (*c.*900), had 17. At the same period in England, York may have had as many as 30 altars.

Over a century later, a set of religious regulations was enshrined with the *Regularis Concordia*, introduced as part of a national monastic reform policy. Significantly, the *Concordia* introduced two new religious observations. These were the 'Office for All Saints' and the 'Office for the Dead'. The text also referred to private prayers within separate chapels, stating that 'after these they [the monks] shall go to matins of all Saints singing an antiphon in honour of the saint to whom the chapel to which they are bound is dedicated: there follows lauds for the dead' (*Concordia*: 20). The *Concordia* also refers to the use of the Trental of St Gregory in its memorial liturgy and prayers for the royal house, which may be a further indication of a growing trend for personalised masses. Excavations at Winchester's Old Minster in the 1960s revealed that the church was subject to significant structural changes in the mid-tenth century. Some of these changes may have been contemporary with the writing of the *Concordia* and included the construction of a series of flanking porticus that may indicate an increased structural elaboration in response to liturgical change. Similarly in AD 950, Dunstan added two lateral porticus to his monasteries at Glastonbury and later at Canterbury, and the north porticus at St Laurence's, Bradford-on Avon, has been dated to between 1000 and 1050. The porticus at Breamore appears to be integral with the original build of the church and is dated by an inscription over the porticus arch to the late tenth century. Significantly, one interpretation for the use of this porticus is as a baptistery or as a chapel for private devotion. At Deerhurst, Arnold Klukas has suggested that the *secreti oratorii loci*, or secret places of prayer referred to in the *Concordia*, were actually located in the porticus. Although Klukas suggests that these chapels may have been on the upper floors, the porticus' eastern chapels provide another possibility (7). These chapels were in a sense physically separate from the church, as they were accessed via the north and south porticus, thus providing them with some level of exclusivity and relative detachment. In the tenth-century church at Thorney, founded by Bishop Æthelwold, there is evidence for a former altar in the north porticus. Structural evidence for subsidiary altars in porticus of this period can also be found at Beverley, Hexham and Rochester, for example. At Deerhurst, the north porticus has evidence for aumbries, or liturgical cupboards, associated with former altars. At Britford, the portal to the north porticus contains elaborately carved panels (especially when compared to the rather rustic example on the south side). Such decoration may suggest that this particular area of the church was of some specific importance. Indeed Yorke has suggested that it may be evidence of patronage by the Wessex royal family and if this is true, then it may have served as some form of memorial chapel, or at the very least any activity carried out within was linked to the royal family through architectural patronage.

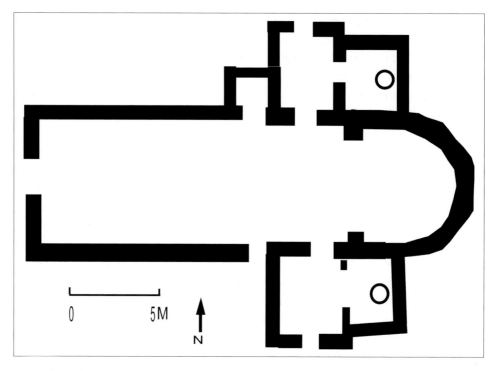

7 Deerhurst showing location of 'secret' chapels

INTERCESSION AND THE LOCAL CHURCH IN ANGLO–NORMAN ENGLAND

By the turn of the eleventh century there were many diverse forms of ecclesiastical establishment in England. Many of the former minster houses, once institutionally independent, were now a key component of Anglo-Saxon rural administration. However, since the tenth-century reforms, religious practice within the monastic or minster churches had become increasingly exclusive and less accessible to the majority of the laity. These churches were also responsible for increasingly large areas of parochial control and pastoral care and as a result were becoming more and more estranged from many medieval communities, a pattern specifically noticed in Hampshire by Patrick Hase. As a result, the less wealthy classes in particular looked for more accessible and intimate contexts for religious and memorial practice. One such context that emerged during this period was the medieval guild, a collective society of merchants and tradesmen. As well as being concerned with the development of craft skills, regulations and mercantile interests, many guilds also had a responsibility for their members' spiritual welfare, both in life and in death. For example, the tenth-century guild at Exeter retained its own mass priest and its statutes refer to the special emphasis placed on worship and prayer. They also state that when any brother died, every member was obliged to perform special devotions for the departed soul. In this sense, all guilds have been described as 'burial societies'. At Bedwyn, the guild statutes stated that if any members died, five masses or five psalters were to be celebrated for the good of their souls. The formation of guilds from as early as the tenth century indicates an increasing lay responsibility for the provision of intercession strategies.

A particularly significant development that was to change the nature of lay religious practice dramatically was the rapid proliferation of local or 'private' churches built by wealthy individuals, which emerged noticeably from the ninth century onwards. This type of church was identified in the early eleventh-century code of King Æthelred II, which indicated that below the status of the great and the lesser minsters or monasteries, there was a range of local proprietary churches, often with independent burial rights. These churches took many forms. Some, such as Earls Barton and Portchester, contained towers with a possible chapel on one floor and secular accommodation on another. Others, perhaps the majority, were basic single or double-celled structures, such as the surviving examples at Alton Barnes and Corhampton (*8*) and the excavated examples at Raunds and Wharram Percy (*colour plate 1*). These local churches were almost certainly status symbols of local elites. However, they were more closely associated with the local

8 Anglo-Saxon church, Corhampton. Note 'porticus' and brick east end of chancel are Victorian additions

settlement than many minster churches, and therefore provided the community with a potentially more direct and regular contact with religious practice. They were also an important component of many urban landscapes; Winchester for example, had around 50 such churches by 1100, and London perhaps as many as 100.

These local churches, often located in or close to a settlement, provided a place for communal worship for their owners and more personal contact with the priest, who was often hired to pray for the soul of the proprietor. It is significant that the excavated private churches at Faccombe Netherton, Goltho and Trowbridge were located on the boundaries between the manorial estate and settlement, suggesting the churches' physical relationship to both. Such churches were obvious status symbols and became an essential accoutrement of lordly status. However, the relatively large size of many of these churches, such as the surviving examples at Alton Barnes, Boarhunt, Escomb and Corhampton suggests that they were designed to accommodate a significant group of people, likely that of the wider community. Despite the private origins of such foundations, the overall intention was that they were to be used by local communities. Historians Barbara Yorke and John Blair argue that as such they represented a considerable advance in the provision of ecclesiastical structures for humbler people. These local churches catered for the religious needs of their communities with particular immediacy. They also allowed for the formation of strong social relationships within their communities and a more intimate interaction between the living and their dead through shared memorial and ritual. The masses celebrated within such churches – churches founded by local lay lords, primarily for the good of their souls as well as for local status – were by association intercessory and memorial foundations. A precedent for this had already been set, for example by King Cnut, who in 1020 ordered the building of a church at Ashingdon for the souls of men slain in battle.

Over time, the acquisition of burial rights also bound the living and the dead physically, and the communal graveyards that many of the later churches were to provide perpetuated the memory of the community's dead. The local church was therefore a monument of collective community memory in a way that the minster churches could never be.

THE LOCAL CHURCH IN THE TWELFTH CENTURY

The Norman Conquest of England in the late eleventh century introduced widespread changes both in central government and within ecclesiastical administration. It also initiated the so-called great rebuilding of many timber churches to stone, which also provided a more practical opportunity for structural expansion. The Conquest arguably acted as a catalyst in forming closer ties with the continent and facilitated the institutional reforms that were spreading across Europe. It also heralded the introduction of new monastic orders which enabled lesser nobility to become monastic patrons, such as the Augustinians and Cluniacs who flooded into England within a few years of the Conquest. In England, the late eleventh and early twelfth centuries also witnessed a series of institutional changes that dramatically changed the nature of lay church ownership. A series of reforms championed the moral superiority of the church and sought to liberate the clergy from dependence on the laity. Thus by the end of the twelfth century secular lords were perceived more as patrons of their churches, with right of presentation, than direct overlords and proprietors. During this period, many formerly 'private' churches were presented as gifts to monastic houses. Here it was also likely that intercessory motives were a factor behind the giving of such gifts. The Augustinian canons, for example, were a major beneficiary – these priests had an institutional duty to perform regular masses, many of which were celebrated in the side chapels of these new monastic houses.

In the twelfth century, many of the English nobility were also once again founding monastic institutions with the specific aim of individual memorial. For example, the church of St Katherine's by the Tower founded in London by Queen Mathilda in 1148, was served by a master, brothers and a number of poor whose sole duty was to offer up prayers and attend masses for the souls of the Queen's two children. Similarly, the Bishop of Winchester, Henry of Blois, founded a house of chaplains at Marwell to sing masses for his soul sometime after 1128. In the late eleventh century, the church of Stoke St Nectan was served by 12 canons, each apparently supported by his own endowment. These developments may suggest a growing concern for a more direct and formal intercession. However, for those slightly lower down the social order, the local or parish church may still have offered a more practical alternative. David Crouch has suggested that one of the earliest chantry foundations may have been that founded by Roger Rustein at Snettisham church around 1193.

By the end of the twelfth century, the local church had become fully institutionalised and we see the emergence of the parish church as an institutional component of late medieval society. Significantly, it is also this period that witnessed widespread additions to parish church fabric in the form of aisles which may have been intended to provide additional space for subsidiary altars and by the end of the twelfth century, most parish churches were provided with at least one aisle. Like the earlier porticus, the function of the aisle has been the subject of much debate. Most commonly, aisles have been interpreted as a response to demographic changes and, more likely, as a major response to developments in liturgy, a view supported by church archaeologist Richard Morris. They may also represent the emergence of the local parish as a formal collective entity that facilitated the raising of parochial finance and the ability to build and embellish the churches. In this case, aisles could function as a communal amenity. The function of aisles, together with the fact that they do not appear earlier – generally no earlier than the twelfth century in most parish churches – may also suggest a lay reaction to contemporary proprietary changes noted above, and the continued influence of the wealthy laity on the fabric of a crystallising parish church. Many aisles were added to parish churches in the late twelfth century. In Hampshire, for example, 11 out of 17 recently studied churches had aisles by 1200. Over half of these were initially singular additions. Elsewhere, in a study of Worcestershire churches in the twelfth century, C.J. Bond has identified the construction of at least 13 single aisles in the parish churches of this period.

It is unlikely, as might at first glance seem reasonable, that the introduction of the aisle was the result of demographic change. Demographic change would occur gradually over a longer period and be more noticeable in some areas than others, particularly urban areas. In London, for example, where demographic changes were more acute, work by John Schofield has suggested that there is evidence for only one church having an aisle added in the twelfth century. It is also important to remember that as well as expanding church space, aisles also dramatically affected the liturgical integrity of the church, for first and foremost this was still religious space. Significantly, the addition of a single aisle to many parish churches is contemporary with the growing limitations set on lay influence on the local church. The introduction of aisles as a structural (often single) addition to church fabric occurred at a time when the changes wrought by various church reforms were coming to fruition. This might be suggestive of the redirection of lay influence upon the church, manifested in a distinctly private acquisition of religious space in the form of the aisle. If so, then the aisle may have been a compromise between lay proprietary desires and the clerical domination of an increasingly institutionalised church. It is therefore likely that the changes to the layout of many churches of this period reflected the maintenance of physical contexts for personalised memorial practice coupled with available opportunity. The emergence of the new institutionalised parish church and a move away from the lay-owned local or private churches now meant that new strategies for memorial practice had to be devised.

Thus, the second half of the twelfth century heralded a series of major changes that radically altered the form and fabric of the local church. The addition of aisles to many parish churches of the period was influenced by similar developments occurring in greater monastic houses some decades earlier. Structural changes to both the fabric and internal organisation of the parish church coincided with a series of ecclesiastical reforms affecting lay proprietary concerns. These factors above all else (including demographic factors) could explain the introduction and function of aisles founded within such a relatively short space of time (and well after they first appeared in monastic houses). However, if aisles represent an appropriation of parish church space for memorial practice then how was this actually enacted? Here, the spatial analysis of the aisle and its relationship to the rest of church space, especially the chancel – the site of the high altar which was the principal focus of the church – may shed some light on its function. Although the doctrine of transubstantiation was not officially recognised until 1215, the twelfth century witnessed the increasing popularity of the mass as an important component of lay piety. As mentioned earlier, a particularly important component of the mass was visual communion with the Elevation of the Host. This generally took place at the high altar within the east end, or chancel, of the church. It would seem important, therefore, for church space to facilitate a clear view of the high altar for the laity. Despite this, the analysis of former visual relationships between aisle and chancels suggests that often the high altar was visually separated from the aisles. However, an altar within the aisle itself may have provided an alternative or subsidiary ritual focus. The survival of twelfth-century piscinas in some churches, such as at Niton, St Ives, St Martin's in Canterbury and at Tarrant Hinton, suggests the associated presence of altars in the aisles at this time. At Bishops Cannings the south aisle gives the impression of a distinct liturgical area with minimal visual relationship to the chancel. Analysis of the churches at Aldbourne, Cheddar, Stoke d'Abernon (*9*) and Wharram Percy (*10*) – all of which saw aisles constructed in the twelfth century – shows that the aisles, and any later chapels and transepts, had a limited visual relationship to the high altar. Again this suggests not only the presence of individual subsidiary altars but also their relative importance to religious practice. The examination of visual relationships between aisles and high altars strongly indicates that in these cases the devotional focus may have been within the aisles themselves and probably against the east wall. The presence of an altar within the aisle of a church is a major feature of later parish churches, as is the position of chantries proper within aisles. In these cases chantries and, as we shall see in later chapters, squints (small internal windows) were often used to facilitate lines of sight between chapel altars and the high altar. Significantly, the twelfth-century squint between the aisle and chancel at Compton certainly suggests the former presence of an aisle altar here at this period (*60*).

Furthermore, the restricted location of such altars, possibly set aside for an exclusive group of people, a family or even a guild or fraternity, suggests that the altars were a collective focus. At St Martin's, Wharram Percy, the addition

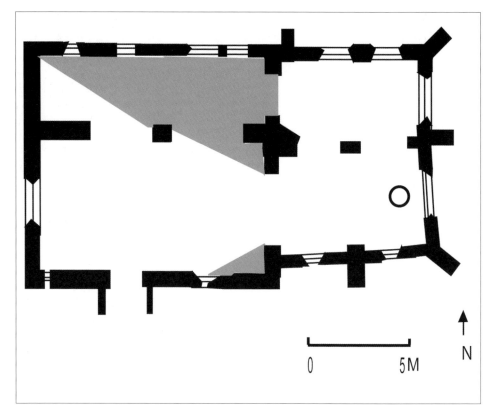

9 St Mary's Stoke d'Abernon. Visual relationships between north aisle (*c.*1190) and chancel

of an aisle took place in the late twelfth century, a period particularly associated with the influence of the Norman Percy family. The aisle extended eastward far beyond the view of the chancel. In fact, it appears that the east end of the south aisle bears no liturgical relationship to the chancel whatsoever. It can therefore be suggested that this space was a separate liturgical area with its own altar. Taking into account its association with the Percys and the significant proprietary changes of the time, it can be conjectured that this was a space dedicated for the use of the lord and his family for prayer. In relation to this, architectural similarities have been noted between this significant phase of construction in the church and work done on the associated manor house, including the identifiable work of the same mason, which may further indicate direct lay influence.

Archaeological examination of church fabric can present evidence for a series of related changes in church design that seem, to a certain degree, to have their motivation in an increasing need to develop more personalised strategies for

10 Wharram Percy church, showing the remains of the former Norman arcade in the south wall and the remains of the south aisle in the foreground

intercession and piety in periods of doctrinal and institutional change. Though the term 'chantry' is mainly used in the context of the mid-thirteenth century onward, it can be seen that the constituents of such a phenomenon, and the directing motivations behind it, lie in a series of causes and effects inherent within the origins and evolution of the English church in the early medieval period. Generally speaking these early foundations contained the criteria for what would later be reflected, albeit in microcosmic form, in the foundation of the later medieval chantry. The evolution of the chantry evolved hand-in-hand with significant developments between church and community, as reflected in church topography and fabric. It is thus clear that to some extent beliefs in the afterlife influenced the development of the church in early medieval England. Notions of purgatory were simultaneously evolving at this time, but lacked any clear doctrinal definition or clarification. This had changed by the thirteenth century, a period that saw the first firmly-documented chantry chapels. Having considered the background of early memorial and intercessory practice from a largely archaeological perspective, we will now move on to examine perceptions of the afterlife in the late medieval period and the related emergence of more formalised strategies for the afterlife.

CHAPTER 4

LATE MEDIEVAL STRATEGIES FOR INTERCESSION

This chapter will discuss the development of purgatorial doctrine and related religious practice from the twelfth century onwards and consider the various strategies for intercession which consequently emerged at this time. It will thus provide a framework for the more detailed analysis of specific types of chantry chapel, their form, fabric and spatial considerations, in subsequent chapters.

By the late twelfth century, the concept of purgatory was formally recognised and had become part of the official 'language' of the western church. Indeed, it is only from this period that we first see the use of the noun *puragtorium* as a definitive classification. This has led some scholars, such as Jacques le Goff, to suggest that this period witnessed the 'birth of purgatory' as a clearly defined and universally accepted concept. This, it should be noted, has been refuted by others, such as Richard Southern, who are unhappy with the linguistic basis of such interpretations. Whatever the true origins of the formal definition, this period certainly witnessed doctrinal developments that offered more coherent means of dealing with the penances attached to sin. These developments, it may be argued, gave a more structured and legal framework for intercessory practice. In the thirteenth century, two church councils had a direct effect on penitential liturgy and intercessory practice. In 1215, the Fourth Lateran Council proclaimed that everyone who had attained a responsible age was bound to confess their sins at least once a year to their parish priest, and to receive the Eucharist. The extent to which the former was actually carried out regularly is open to debate, but it is likely that Easter provided one formal opportunity. We also know from some contemporary documents, such as the churchwardens' accounts of St Mary-at-Hill, London, that chantry priests were drafted in at these busy times, probably to help at mass and to facilitate confession. A second Council, at Lyon in 1274, provided a formal and institutional recognition of purgatory as a place 'that the souls, by the purifying compensation, are purged after death'.

From the thirteenth century there were various attempts to introduce a more conscious mapping of purgatory and an endeavour to locate it in space and time. Thomas Aquinas (who died en route to the Council at Lyon) claimed that the actual location of purgatory was below the earth and was in direct proximity to Hell, a view similar to that upheld several centuries later in the *Lytel Boke* of 1532. In some sources, the close relationship between Hell and purgatory was implicit – in the *Ordynace of Chrysten Men* of 1502, purgatory was claimed to have been part of Hell. It is clear, however, that throughout the medieval period the location of purgatory was subject to various interpretations and its precise location was never actually confirmed by the church. As the Jesuit William Allen remarked in the late sixteenth century, it was better to be in doubt of its precise location than to 'stande in contentious reasoning of thinges uncertain' (Allen, 1565). What was important was that it existed and that mechanisms for its transgression were in place and enshrined in church doctrine.

PURGATORY AND BURIAL CUSTOM

The twelfth and thirteenth centuries, then, witnessed more formal developments in beliefs surrounding purgatory and related intercession. They also coincided with significant changes in burial practice. Archaeologist Dawn Hadley has noted a so-called burial shift occurring in churchyard burial, where evidence suggests that less care was taken in terms of preservation of the buried body than in earlier periods. Excavations at St Helens-on-the-Walls in York and at Kellington, for example, have shown that prior to the twelfth century, more care was taken to make sure that burials were not disturbed by later interments. After this period, the evidence suggests that graves were often freely disturbed by building works and later burials. At Raunds Furnells, many of the earlier graves, dating to the ninth or tenth centuries, were marked. By the twelfth century, however, there was a more random distribution of graves, suggesting that markers were no longer important. These changes may reflect a shift in beliefs concerning the afterlife and the influence of purgatorial belief in the twelfth and thirteenth centuries – emphasis was placed on the welfare of the soul and not the earthly remains. Prior to the twelfth century, it may have been important to allow the corporeal remains to survive intact for the perceived eventual Day of Judgement when, as the Athanasian Creed of the first millennium claims, all men must rise with their bodies and are to render an account of their deeds.

This was taken literally and may be one of the reasons behind burial orientation in Christian cemeteries with the head to the west, allowing the corpse to stand up and face east when revived on the Day. A derivation of this can be found in some priestly burials of the period, such as that at St Peter's in Barton-on-Humber, excavated by Warwick and Kirsty Rodwell. Here a priest was buried, complete with chalice and patten, and orientated west–east so as to enable him to rise up and face his congregation at the prescribed time.

The period between the tenth and twelfth centuries also witnessed a range of different burial customs, possibly linked to changing beliefs in the afterlife. The presence of charcoal in some burials of this period may reflect a desire to mark the location of the body or to provide some form of symbolic purification. Examples have been found at sites such as Old Minster, Winchester and St Nicholas Shambles, London. Charcoal burials may have symbolised the use of ash in traditional acts of penitence as outlined by Daniel 9:3 – 'And I set my face unto the Lord God, to seek by prayer and supplications, with fasting, and sackcloth, and ashes'. Another feature of this period is the presence of stones sometimes found in burials supporting the skull, often referred to as 'pillow stones'. Examples can be found at St Nicholas Shambles and Raunds, among other sites. The standard explanation is that they kept the face upright, so that at Judgement Day, when the body rose from the grave, the resurrected body would automatically face east, looking at the risen Christ. Yet, as archaeologist Chris Daniell has pointed out, the *Chronicon Lemovicense*, dating to around 1170, informs us that when Henry, son of Henry II, lay dying, he had stones placed under his head and feet, together with the more familiar penitential symbols of sack cloth and ashes. Although a singular example (and allowing for the paucity of documents generally during this period) this may suggest that pillow stones served a penitential function in burials and that they were linked to changing beliefs in the afterlife. This may represent an intermediate stage, where the body was treated as a symbol of professed penitence.

From at least the ninth century, grave location was of some importance, particularly with regard to the spatial relationship between place of burial and the church. For example, excavations carried out at North Elmham revealed that the most favoured burial location was as close to the east end of the Anglo-Saxon minster church as possible. This was no doubt because the east end was the setting for the high altar, the prime religious focus of the church. A similar pattern can be seen at Raunds where the earliest burials are clustered close towards the south-east of the church chancel. Later, a favoured location for chantry chapels would be close to high altars or saints' shrines. For the laity in the Anglo-Saxon period, burial inside the church was strictly off-limits, one notable exception being that of Earl Siward in his church of St Olaf in York in

1055. In the following century it was to become more common, particularly for patrons, to be buried within the walls of the church. One major reason behind the inclusion of the dead within the confines of the church walls was that burial liturgies increasingly revolved around the provision for personalised contexts for intercession, particularly through the celebration of masses and dedicated prayers. The symbolic presence of the dead represented by visual memorials and tombs was therefore all-important in evoking and maintaining the memory of the deceased. In 1292, the Statutes of Chichester decreed that no burials were allowed in the church or chancel other than those of lords of the village, patrons of the church or the rector or vicar. The introduction of the decree suggests that this may have become fairly common practice by this date.

By far the most favoured burial location in the church was before the high altar, indicated by the thirteenth-century tomb of King John at Worcester and that of Sir Walter Manny at the Carthusian monastery he founded in London in the fourteenth century. At Etchingham parish church, the Lord of the Manor William de Etchingham, was buried before the high altar within the chancel that he had rebuilt in the 1360s. More dramatically, the tomb of Bishop Gifford of Worcester was erected next to the high altar of the cathedral and set up an intriguing spatial rivalry. However, it was to prove an unpopular choice of location. In 1302, the Archbishop of Canterbury discovered that not only had the tomb displaced that of a local bishop, it also darkened the area of the high altar and the site of St Oswald's shrine.

For the rich and influential, proximity to the shrine of a saint was another favoured tomb location throughout the medieval period. This is particularly well illustrated at Westminster Abbey, where the tombs of the English medieval kings and their queens are clustered around the shrine of St Edward the Confessor. At Canterbury Cathedral, the tomb of Archbishop Hubert Walter (1193-1205) was situated in the south ambulatory of the Trinity chapel, created to house Becket's shrine. The tomb is also believed to have been modelled on Becket's now lost shrine. The relationship of tombs and saints' shrines can also be seen at parish church level where certain members of the laity desired to be buried close to a saint's image or dedicated subsidiary altar. It is important here to remember that, to the medieval mind, the absence of physical relics could be compensated for in the form of sacred images and dedicated altars.

These strategies reveal the deeper underlying individual responses to the afterlife. Here, it may be suggested, certain individuals were attempting to 'tailor' their preparations. For example, excavations at the medieval cemetery of St Mary Spital in London revealed the remains of four individuals who were buried with papal lead seals of the fourteenth century which, according to Geoff Egan of the Museum of London, were once attached to papal indulgences. Egan states that the individuals took their indulgences with them to the grave as proof of purchase of promised remission. One of the burials was tentatively identified as Johanna, wife of the rich mercer William Eynsham, who founded the chantry chapel above the hospital's charnel house.

The emergence of more formal definitions of purgatory, then, meant that bodily preservation was arguably less important than the welfare of one's soul. This welfare was catered for by the creation of certain personalised mechanisms that did not necessarily focus completely on the body, but placed importance on the memory of the individual, facilitated through the foundation of chantry chapels and highly visual monumental tombs.

LATE MEDIEVAL VISIONS OF THE AFTERLIFE

The theme of death dominated the images, literature and liturgy of the late medieval church, from the vividly life-like paintings of the Doom, Last Judgment and the Weighing of Souls through to cadaver tombs and the manuals of the *Ars Moriendi*, instructing the faithful how to make a pious end and provide for a good death. In the late medieval era, much of how one thought and acted was related to a conviction that there was some form of penitential existence after natural death. Buttressed by communal faith systems and church doctrine, it governed and directed to a large extent how people led their lives. Indeed, life was in many ways a preparation for death.

This belief often informed moral themes for associated art forms. For example, at Swanbourne, a wall painting dating to the late fourteenth or early fifteenth century depicted a medieval allegory showing a moralising narrative concerning penitence and the fate of those who died without it. In one panel souls in purgatory are shown pleading for help from living 'friends'. Such help, in the form of prayers, provided a calculable reduction of time spent in purgatory – the more prayers, the less time spent in purgatory. Actions such as the perpetual performance of masses were viewed as being particularly efficacious. These factors, it will be remembered, had emerged several centuries before through the writings of Augustine, Gregory and Bede, and were by now ingrained in the medieval mind.

Although there was never to be any 'official' description of purgatory, the laity were kept fully informed of what could be expected through popular works such as Thomas More's *Supplication of Souls* and St Patrick's *Purgatory*. These texts often took the form of personal 'revelations', such as that of the Monk of Eynsham translated in the late fifteenth century or that of St Bridget of Sweden a century earlier. Many of these works presented an image of purgatory that was threatening and loaded with warning. For example, the twelfth-century St Patrick's *Purgatory* described:

> … an infernal pit, a vast gulf, dark, and emitting an intolerable stench, and full of screaming and howling. By the pit was a serpent of infinite magnitude, bound by a great chain, the one end of which seemed to be fastened in the pit; before the mouth of this serpent stood a multitude of souls, which he sucked in like flies at each breath, and then, with the return of respiration, blew them out scorched to sparks; and this process continued till the souls were purged of their sins.

Fire was a central component of medieval visions of purgatory. In the first decade of the fifteenth century, the Sussex priest Richard Alkerton thoughtfully informs us that the sinful were:

> … boiled in fire and brimstone without end. Venomous worms … shall gnaw all the members unceasingly, and the worms of conscience shall gnaw the soul … Now ye shall have everlasting bitterness … This fire that tormenteth you shall never be quenched, and they that tormenteth you shall never be weary neither die.

In contrast, however, the story of *The Gast of Gy*, possibly of the fourteenth century, presented a purgatory in more humane terms and thus illustrated the descriptive range of purgatorial accounts available to the laity. The *Gast*, a purgatorial spirit, is friendly and tolerant in his dealings with the prior who questions him about purgatory. Unlike other texts, this work is not peppered with gruesome and terrifying imagery designed to warn the reader of the punishments that await. Rather, it presents a more compassionate context in which purgatory is viewed as a doctrine of hope and even comfort; a state where the deceased resided and were prayed for, and importantly a place in which eventual salvation was assured.

From a modern, rationalist perspective, medieval beliefs in the afterlife had two major incentives: the church provided a coherent structure for the afterlife and acted as the only context in which one could secure a quick journey through purgatory and the assurance of eventual salvation; or, more cynically, the whole construction of purgatory and the rites associated with it was a mechanism of institutional control. Here the existence of purgatory offered a dire warning to those who would not fully embrace the church's authority. To some, however, belief in purgatory also offered emotional comfort and existential security. It presented an explanation of what happened after death and, importantly, it offered a medium for the potential of salvation. It was therefore a powerful force and one that was a guiding principle throughout the Middle Ages. Importantly, notions of purgatory led to a realisation that preparations or insurances could be made in this life. Therefore, in the later medieval period, purgatory provided motivation for pilgrimage and various good works and acts of charity. All sought to perform acts of good which would lessen time spent in purgatory and which involved an element of personal sacrifice and hardship. This allowed for the accumulation and storage of merit which helped one in the afterlife. The medieval Yorkshire poem *The Lyke-wake Dirge* makes plain the connection between acts of charity and the eventual fate of the soul should they be neglected. If one fails in the deliverance of acts of charity then one's soul will suffer:

> From the bridge of dread when thou may pass every night and all
> To purgatory fire thou come at last and Christ receive thy soul
> If ever thou gave meat and drink every night and all
> The fire shall never make thee shrink and Christ receive thy soul
> If meat and drink thy never gave every night and all
> The fire will burn thee to the bare bone and Christ receive thy soul.

As the architectural historian Howard Colvin has stated, a substantial part of late medieval economy was connected to the service of the dead. Naturally therefore, beliefs in purgatory provided a prime motive for the large-scale channelling of resources in the direction of the churches and monasteries. This was reflected in medieval wills, for example, which often include bequests to the 'fabric' of churches, as is witnessed in the many structural additions and large-scale rebuilding of parish churches in particular, in the fifteenth and early sixteenth centuries. For example, in large urban churches such as St Bride's in London, St Thomas's in Salisbury and Holy Trinity in Coventry, church space was greatly expanded thanks to the foundation of chantry chapels dedicated to the singing of masses for those in purgatory. The wills also included provision for works of religious art, which adorned the majority of churches in the medieval period.

Artistic representations too, such as wall painting and decorative sculpture and glass, provided a context for the dissemination of didactic and moral themes relating to purgatory and the afterlife. They often provided visual information relating to the afterlife, such as the Doom paintings that could be found in many churches of the period. Commonly these were painted above the chancel arch, such as the still-vivid depictions at South Leigh (*colour plate 2*) and North Leigh churches (*11*), but some were located in the nave, such as that at Oddington. Wherever they were, they were always in full view of the laity. Sometimes related themes acted as a guidance to good works and were ultimately linked to purgatorial belief. One popular theme, enshrined in church dogma, was the

11 Doom painting, North Leigh church. On the right panel, the souls of the sinful can be seen entering the mouth of hell

Seven Corporal Works of Mercy. These 'works' included feeding the hungry, clothing the naked and burying the dead. One of the earliest known depictions of the Works of Mercy, dating to around 1320, comes from Kimpton parish church. Other outstanding examples of depictions of the theme can still be seen adorning the church walls at Pickering and Wickhampton, and it was also a subject of one of the windows in the collegiate chantry of Ralph, Lord Cromwell, at Tattershall. On the west wall of Trotton church, a depiction of a 'good man' (perhaps the donor) is surrounded by the Seven Corporal Works of Mercy. The inclusion of the good man helped illustrate the relationship between goods works and personal destiny, as well as placing the individual in a devotional context that forged a symbolic connection between the individual and the works performed.

By the end of the thirteenth century, any opposition to the notion of purgatory had largely disappeared and its existence was, by and large, accepted. Traditionally, monasteries were the recipients of the lay endowment of memorial and votive masses, normally recorded in calendars and obituary registers. However, developments surrounding intercessory doctrine, facilitated no doubt by the monasteries and the later colleges, began to percolate down to parish level. By the end of the century, the increased privatisation of church space by individuals and collectives reflected a growing demand for private commemoration. It is in this period that we begin to see wide-scale documentary evidence for chantry foundations in churches and monasteries, the physical remains of which provide the major focus of this work. By 1300, many local parish churches were virtually unrecognisable compared with their eleventh and twelfth-century precursors. The addition and expansion of aisles, spacious naves and chancels, light-filled clerestories and ornate side chapels, largely as a result of personal endowments, greatly embellished and expanded church space and fabric and reflected distinct directional changes. There was a shift towards a strategy for a more complex and personalised context for individual piety within the communal context. These changes also bear witness to the inspired development of related artistic media in the multifarious forms of sculpture, painting, stained glass, images, artefacts, hangings and vestments. Belief in purgatory was to provide a lasting source of inspiration throughout the Late Middle Ages, governing to various extents, not just how people led their individual lives, but also how they patronised, decorated and embellished their churches. Furthermore, they reflected a desire to develop more varied expressions of individual piety in the communal context and attested to the importance of the visual arts in the development of strategies for the afterlife.

By the late thirteenth century, the foundation of chantries represented the ultimate personal strategy for intercession: the endowment of a mass and celebrant, often housed within a defined architectural space, the chantry chapel. Some foundations, with their individual altars, tombs and particular architectural styles and decoration (sometimes at variance with the rest of the church) represented a distinct privatisation of church space. However, as will be later shown, such institutions, though individually founded, had a wider part to play in the religious devotions of the community as a whole and they were integral and familiar components of church space and medieval religious experience. There were two major considerations behind the foundation of chantry chapels: form and fabric – their design, decoration and spatial setting; and their internal arrangements and relationships to other important areas of the church. It is these aspects that will be considered in the following chapters, with reference to chapels founded in both religious houses and the parishes.

CHAPTER 5

THE FORM AND FABRIC OF CHANTRY CHAPELS IN RELIGIOUS HOUSES

We will now turn to the chantry chapels themselves and examine the nature and various types of chantry chapel, and the spatial considerations behind their foundation. We will first examine those founded in the religious houses of England from the twelfth century onwards.

The dissolution of the monasteries in the third decade of the sixteenth century and the subsequent despoliation and destruction of many former religious houses meant that the physical survival of chantry chapels in such institutions is rare (*12*). Even those that were fortunate enough to survive were, over time, drastically reordered. For example the 'restorations' at Salisbury Cathedral in the eighteenth century brought about the removal of many of the chapel screens, the transfer of the chantry chapel of Walter Hungerford from the nave to the choir and the destruction of the impressive Hungerford and Beauchamp chapels at the east end of the cathedral church, which were considered to have structurally weakened the cathedral fabric. Had it survived, the Beauchamp chapel in particular would have offered one of the most impressive examples of medieval chantry foundation. Those structures that do survive, such as the monuments still found in many cathedrals and colleges, often offer elaborate and therefore wholly unrepresentative examples. The majority of chantries founded in religious houses of the medieval period were of a more modest nature, consisting, in many cases, of an endowment of a pre-existing altar. Even where survival was not an issue, these have left no archaeological trace. Yet the impressive monuments found in many cathedrals and collegiate chapels can still offer a precious insight into the nature of such foundations as established by the higher echelons of medieval society.

12 Monastic ruins, Byland

Most monasteries of the medieval period owed their origin to wealthy patrons. Implicit within such foundations was the requirement that members of the religious community would pray for the founder's soul. At the Augustinian Abbey of Bristol, for example, the soul of the twelfth-century founder, Robert Fitzharding, was still commemorated by the community in the decades before its dissolution in the sixteenth century. The Augustinian order was a particularly popular choice among many founders and benefactors in the twelfth century. One reason was their status as priests, as well as monks, a status which ordained that they celebrate mass once a day. The particular requirements of the canons themselves may therefore have encouraged the endowment of personal masses by the laity. By the end of the twelfth century, around 100 Augustinian houses had been founded, including the first foundation at Colchester and the important London houses of Holy Trinity, Aldgate, St Bartholomew-the-Great, Smithfield and Southwark Priory.

By 1300, monastic patronage had moved from the founding of religious houses to more personal endowments, a trend that undoubtedly had been influenced by emerging doctrines relating to purgatory and penitential liturgy and the resultant emergence of the chantry as a personalised and intimate strategy for the afterlife. The first recorded formal chantry was that of Bishop Hugh of Wells in Lincoln Cathedral sometime around 1235, but it is likely that there were similar, undocumented institutions founded prior to that date. Liturgies concerned with intercession and the fate of individual souls may have also gained particular momentum with the generous and well-spread endowments provided by Edward I to commemorate the death of Queen Eleanor in 1290. As well as the twelve memorial crosses erected for her in the places where her funeral cortège rested en route to Westminster and the provision for masses at York and elsewhere, a chantry was founded for her at Harby in Nottinghamshire, where she died. Eleanor's funeral at Westminster was an elaborate and very public event. Afterwards, 30 great candles were placed on her tomb. Henceforth every abbot was to perform a commemorative mass on the anniversary of her death, a practice that continued until the Reformation. Such an important and highly public event was an exemplary model for wider commemorative practice.

The foundation of a chantry was out of reach for the majority of the laity unless they were part of a guild or fraternity. One cheaper option was the 'obit': the reading out of the names of the deceased on the anniversary of their death. Many of the obits were written down and kept in a monastery's *Liber Vitae* (Book of Life) or Obit Book. A surviving example is the Obit Book of Hereford Cathedral. Here the majority of the obit entries were inscribed in black ink, providing an indelible record of the deceased. However, as over time the pages of the book were filled with hundreds of names, individual entries threatened to drown in a sea of script. Yet the names of the more worthy could still be made to stand out: the entries for bishops and for the more 'deserving' members of the cathedral community (i.e. the most generous) were written in red, while two royal entries are in gold leaf – that for Queen Philippa and that for Queen Anne and Richard II. The laity could also be 'joined with' monastic communities through becoming a *confrater* or *familiaris*. The *confrater* derived spiritual benefit from the relationship, while the religious house profited from the layperson's gifts. In some instances, the *confrater* could join the community when he or she was close to death. A record of *confraters* and benefactors was probably kept in every religious house in England.

Throughout the medieval period, less wealthy benefactors could still receive prayers from monastic communities by donating gifts or providing a major endowment towards building projects. In 1393, John Wrighte, janitor of the Augustinian priory of St Bartholomew's in Smithfield, London, bequeathed to the church a vestment for the celebration of masses, 26s 8d for the making of a dorsal for the high altar and a chalice of silver gilt. As well as this a penny each was to go to a thousand poor persons, besides other bequests to secular chaplains to pray for his soul. In the fifteenth century, the will of Hugh Atte Fenne requested burial in the chancel of the church of 'Havyngby', Norfolk. He bequeathed to the prior of St Bartholomew's £15 and also paid one penny to every London priest to pray for his soul on the day of his death or the day after. He also willed that masses be sung in the churches of the priories of St John's in Clerkenwell, the Charterhouse and St Bartholomew's in Smithfield, and in the parish churches of St Sepulchre, St Andrew's in Holborn and St Botolph's in Aldersgate, also in London. In addition, Atte Fenne left 100s to St Bartholomew's hospital and a further sum was given to the poor for attending the service at St Bartholomew's. Such strategies indicate the length testators went to to secure vast amounts of prayers.

By the fourteenth century, for those who could afford it, the pre-eminent strategy for the afterlife was the chantry chapel. The foundation of chantry chapels during this period influenced the development of many monastic churches and cathedrals and became an important and influential component in the plan of many religious houses. The establishment of the chantries themselves and the construction and decoration of chantry chapels did much to influence traditional church layout and architectural style, and also shaped developments in related liturgy. The redesigning and rebuilding of many monastic and cathedral churches of the period was intended to provide extra space for chantry foundation – a no doubt lucrative addition to many churches. The eastern arm of the Augustinian house of Christchurch Priory was rebuilt and extended in the fifteenth century and provided ample space for the foundation of chantry chapels. Many of these subsequent foundations remain, particularly the impressive Salisbury, Berkeley and Harys chapels (*colour plate 3*). Another example is Salisbury Cathedral, where the architectural historian Sarah Brown has noted that the plan of the new cathedral in the early thirteenth century incorporated a second pair of transepts and thus increased the space available for chapels. At the Cistercian abbey of Byland (*12*), the mid-thirteenth century witnessed the removal of the lay brothers' choir stalls and the reorganisation of this area to provide extra space for the foundation of chantries. Such spaces were in a sense 'ripe' for the endowment of masses, and the foundation of chantries and chapels may have been provided 'to order'. The huge popularity of chantry foundation was also a major influence on the growth of priestly ordinations. For example, by the fifteenth century, the chantry priests of London outnumbered the parish incumbents by nearly three to one.

ACCOMMODATION

Continuous foundations by gifts and bequests created a large body of clergy who, by the fifteenth century at least, formed an important element of cathedral clerical staff. At York Minster, for example, there were nearly 50 chantries and at Lincoln Cathedral around 30. The duties of the chantry priest, as set out by the terms on which their chantries had been founded, often included attendance at some of the rites and observations of the cathedral. They were in many cases explicitly subject to the jurisdiction of the dean and chapter. Furthermore, the property and advowsons (right of appointment) of chantries were frequently bestowed by the founders on the dean and chapter, in trust, always on the payment of chaplains or a chaplain. The number of chantry priests attached to monastic communities encouraged the foundation of communal accommodation, or colleges, which in some instances formed part of the original chantry endowment. These various ranks of clergy lived a communal collegiate life in buildings or houses close to the church. In the majority of monasteries and cathedrals, chantry priests were part of the monastic community and therefore were lodged in the buildings of the monastic precinct. However, the situation in the secular cathedrals, such as Exeter, London, Salisbury and York, for example, was different. Here there were no monks to live communally within the confines of the cloister, but canons, who resided separately in the cathedral closes and outer precincts. Many chantries were founded with separate accommodation, but over time, and when such institutions had reached a critical mass, 'colleges' emerged, i.e. residential communities for the use of chantry priests and other members of the minor clergy. Eventually the chantry priests, vicars choral and the rest of the clerical body associated with private masses and intercession formed a large element of the secular cathedral community. They came to be 'cloistered' in their own accommodation within the cathedral precinct. At Exeter, the close surrounding the cathedral contained houses built for the canons as well as halls for the chantry priests and vicars choral. Exeter's small college built to accommodate the chantry priests in the early sixteenth century stood on the north side of the cathedral close; fragments of the college still survive in later housing. The relatively large cathedral closes of the secular cathedrals, such as Wells and Salisbury, provided ample space for the accommodation of chantry priests, who often lived in their own well-appointed houses. At St Paul's Cathedral in London a dwelling for the chaplain or chaplains was often part of the endowment of a chantry and as a result several 'colleges' or communal dwellings emerged. These colleges, often referred to as 'priesthouses', such as that dedicated to St Peter, were often closely regulated corporate institutions managed by a cathedral warden or 'proctor'. In 1391, for example, Bishop Robert Braybrook of St Paul's ordered that all cathedral chantry priests who did not belong to a cathedral college should take their food in the hall of the 'Presteshous' and that the dean and chapter should allot chambers to as many of them as possible. Other chantry priests dwelling in the grounds of the cathedral served Holmes' College, founded by Adam of Bury, once mayor of London, who had built a chapel of the Holy Ghost to the north of St Paul's. Adam's executor Roger Holmes, a cathedral canon, devised the college's statutes which ruled that every member of the college must swear to be faithful to the community and to 'keep the secrets of its hall'. He also ordained that every year the seven priests should choose one of their number to preside over the others and that each priest should also subscribe a fixed sum for the maintenance of their common meals.

FORM AND FABRIC

Late medieval chantries were therefore an integral element of monastic churches both in terms of clergy and within church space and liturgy. The masses performed at the various chantries formed an important addition to church services and introduced an element of diversity to the forms of Eucharistic practice. For example, detailed instructions for the chantry priests of the Dominican Friary in York survive and concern two perpetual chantries founded by Nicholas and Margaret Blackburn; in one, the chantry of St Mary Magdalene, the celebrating priest was to begin his chantry service by ringing the chapter bell, just as was done for high mass. Every day a mass was to be said for Nicholas while he lived and a Requiem mass for the souls of himself and his wife after their death. Furthermore, at the high altar of the friary church, a mass of the Blessed Virgin Mary was to be celebrated daily followed by specified psalms and prayers. An annual obit was also to be celebrated by the choir, with offices on the feast of St James (25 July) and a Requiem mass on the feast of St Anne (26 July). The obit was to be publicly announced by the city bellman. Many churches had similar arrangements that made the regulated and frequent schedules of liturgical practice numerous and diverse.

The physical impact of chantry foundation in the religious houses could take many forms. The most common was an endowment of a mass to be performed at a pre-existing altar for a set amount of time. At the Benedictine nunnery of Nunnaminster, Winchester, a chantry was founded in 1328 at the altar of St Peter at the east end of the south choir aisle by Robert de Wambergh, Archdeacon of Wells. In 1488, Elizabeth Uvedale was buried at Greyfriars, London, in a raised tomb under the window at the altar of St Mary, close to the tomb of her father, Henry Norbury, which stood between

13 Etching of Salisbury Cathedral in the eighteenth century by Jacob Schnebbelie showing former Hungerford (r) and Beauchamp (l) chapels at east end

14 Etching of Salisbury Cathedral in the eighteenth century by Jacob Schnebbelie detailing interior view of Beauchamp chapel

the altars of St Mary and Holy Cross. She endowed a perpetual chantry here, bequeathing a cope made from her own blue velvet gown, and a chasuble of her tawny velvet gown, for the use of the church. She also bequeathed a chalice of silver gilt, weight 30 ounces, and two cruets of silver, weight 80 ounces, to serve at the altar before which she was buried, presumably that endowed with the chantry.

Other chantries were often founded in pre-existing chapels, such as those at Durham Cathedral founded by Bishop Neville (*c.*1457) in the Galilee chapel and Prior Frosser in the north transept (*c.*1374). Some chapels were also constructed underground in crypts, such as that of Edward the Black Prince (founded *c*.1363) in the crypt at Canterbury. Other cathedral chantry foundations provided structural additions to church fabric. At Thetford Priory, the Howard chapel was built in the angle between the north transept and nave. At Salisbury Cathedral, the chapels of Robert, Lord Hungerford and Bishop Beauchamp were constructed on the outside of the cathedral against the walls of the Trinity chapel (*13, 14*). Nothing survives of these buildings now except the doorway and a decorated canopy from the Beauchamp chapel, though eighteenth-century drawings of the chapels show that they were imposing additions, particularly the chapel of Bishop Beauchamp on the south side of the chapel, with an ogee-arched

15 The Draper chantry chapel, Christchurch Priory

vault and sumptuous internal decoration. It has been suggested by archaeologist Andrew Reynolds that the chancel screen at Compton Bassett – an inordinately fine screen for an otherwise fairly ordinary parish church – may have originally come from one of these chapels.

Many chantry chapels in religious houses appropriated existing space in the main body of the church. A simple arrangement was often to seal off the end of an aisle with a masonry screen, such as the Draper chapel at Christchurch Priory (*15*). In some instances a wooden screen was used, such as the ornately carved and galleried screen to Bishop Langton's chapel in the south aisle at Winchester (*16*). At Durham Cathedral, the Neville chantry screened off a large

16 Langton
chapel,
Winchester
Cathedral

17 Vaughan chapel, St David's Cathedral

portion of the nave's south aisle. On some occasions however, chantry chapels were founded in more practical and less invasive areas of the church. The chantry chapel of Bishop Edward Vaughan at St David's Cathedral was founded (*c.*1520s) in what was formerly, and unusually, a rubbish-strewn open courtyard between the presbytery and Lady Chapel (*17*).

Church space was also effectively enclosed by the use of so-called 'stone-cage chantries', largely dating to the fifteenth and sixteenth centuries. These structures literally 'caged' off areas of the church and contained endowed altars enclosed by a masonry superstructure, often highly decorated with religious and secular motifs. Outstanding examples include those of the bishops of Winchester at Winchester Cathedral (*colour plate 4*), the Berkeley and Salisbury chapels at Christchurch Priory and the Audley chapel at Salisbury (*18*). Many of these chantries also contained tombs and connected vestries, like Bishop Fox's chantry (*c.*1520s) at Winchester. Perhaps one of the most impressive examples of this form is that containing the tomb of Henry VII's son Prince Arthur at Worcester Cathedral. The chantry was built two years after the

18 Audley
chapel,
Salisbury
Cathedral

prince's death in 1504. Inside the chapel there is a lierne (or stellar) vault and a magnificent decorated reredos with its defaced images in canopied niches. The tomb of the prince is situated in the centre of the chapel. Recent archaeological survey using ground-penetrating radar identified the possible grave of the prince a short distance from the tomb itself.

Many chantry chapels, especially those founded within the ambulatories of churches, were encased with wooden screens or iron railings. At Salisbury Cathedral, the chapel of Walter Hungerford, originally in the nave north aisle but now in the choir south aisle, was defined by iron rails. In the cathedral at Durham, contemporary accounts reveal that the fourteenth-century Neville chantry had an 'iron grait' and was partly 'invyroned with iron'. The chantry chapel of Hugh of Gloucester at St Alban's Abbey contained an iron grille, barring it off from the south ambulatory.

In some instances the construction of a new chantry chapel may have destroyed an earlier monument. The chapel of William Wykeham probably replaced an earlier altar to the Virgin Mary in the nave's south arcade at Winchester (*19*) and the chapel of Henry VII certainly superseded an earlier Lady Chapel. At St Alban's the site reserved for the tomb of Abbot John Wheathampstead was appropriated as a chantry chapel for Humphrey, Duke of Gloucester in the 1440s. At Westminster Abbey, the chapel of John Islip (d.1532) appropriated and sectioned off the chapel of St John the Evangelist situated in the south of the north transept. In some instances, earlier foundations were supplemented by later endowments, which in some cases led to rebuilding or enlargement of the chapel. At the collegiate church of Southwell the chantry chapel of Hugh de Vavasour (*c.*1280) was re-endowed and enlarged by the Archbishop of York, William Booth (1452-64). It seems that this family had a particular affiliation to Southwell, as Booth's brother, Lawrence of Durham, and later York, endowed two more chantry foundations in the chapel.

While chapels were constructed for the benefit of the dead, they also benefited the benefactor whilst alive, as they could be used as private pews. The Fox chantry at Winchester was used by the elderly Bishop in the years leading up to his death, as was the chapel of Bishop Audley at Salisbury. At Southwark Cathedral, Amantis Berthelette, the publisher of the English poet John Gower's *Confessio*, recounts that regular masses were said for the soul of the poet before his actual death. It is also possible that Gower's tomb itself was actually constructed and in place by then. The tomb of the living founder may often have been constructed before death; it would act as a powerful *memento mori*, a vivid reminder of death and the need for expiation.

The presence of three squints in the Berkeley chapel at Christchurch Priory, angled to give a view from the western part of the chapel, may suggest that individuals other than the priest would have been present in this chapel. At Tewkesbury Abbey the cage chapel sandwiched within the arcade of the choir north aisle was built in memory of Richard Beauchamp by his wife Isabel Despenser. Begun in 1422 and finished sometime around 1438, the chapel is two-storied; the upper floor was possibly a private pew for Lady Isabel and may once have contained images of the kneeling figures of Isabel and her two husbands. Traces of medieval wall paint remain throughout the chapel.

Many chantry chapels, particularly the free-standing cage chapels, made highly visual statements of piety, status and self-importance. One of the earliest surviving

19 'Stone-cage' chantry chapel of Bishop William Wykeham, Winchester Cathedral

cathedral chantries is that of Bishop Giles de Bridport in Salisbury Cathedral (*20*). The monument dates to around 1260 and is mentioned in the *Valor Ecclesiasticus* of the 1530s as being one of the poorest by that time. Nevertheless, it is highly prominent and visually impressive, and much emphasis was placed on decoration. The tomb stands within a large decorated ogee arch with interior vaulting. Eight narrative reliefs on the exterior illustrate episodes in the life of the Bishop. There is no surviving evidence for an altar; however, a double aumbry survives to the east, suggesting that the chantry mass was likely to have been performed at an altar close by. By the fifteenth century, Salisbury Cathedral may have had as many as 24 such chantries operating within its walls.

Often, chapels were emblazoned with heraldic devices of the founders. Some used playful motifs, or pictograms, which played on the founder's name. Bishop Alcock's chantry in the north-east corner of the presbytery at Ely Cathedral, for example, was decorated with the rebus 'cock'. The Bishop's motto, *Gratia Dei sum quod sum*, appears over the door and on the exterior. On the north side of the presbytery of St Albans' is the chantry chapel of Abbot Ramryge, built about 1522 (*21*). The chapel is highly decorated with secular as well as religious motifs. At the east end of the chapel are shields with the saltire of St Alban, the crowns of St Oswin and the lions of St Amphibal, with niches for the respective figures. The west end the chapel features the arms of St Alban and Ramryge himself. In the panels on the lower part of the south face of the chapel is a series of shields supported by rams holding croziers with the letters RYGE on their collars. Above this a cornice runs around the chapel inscribed with shields that refer to the various cells of the monastery and include Binham, Hertford, Pembroke, Redbourne, Tynemouth and Wymondham priories. Unhappily, the arms of Henry VIII, who dissolved the chapel several years later, were also displayed. Above the shields is an inscription, beginning at the south-east corner of the chapel, taken from the Salisbury Missal, being part of a sequence and antiphon of the psalms.

Sculptured images and paintings of saints and religious events were a feature of many chantry chapels. Such imagery should not be viewed as mere decoration or didactic ornamentation; in many ways it was visible proof of the presence of saints and their intercessory powers. The survival of many elaborate niches in such chapels is indicative of the importance of images, such as the carved reredoses from the Audley chapel in Salisbury and that of Prince Arthur at Worcester Cathedral. In the chantry of John Speke in Exeter Cathedral (*c.*1517), a carved wooden image of Flemish workmanship of St Anne with the Virgin and Child bears witness to the high quality of craftsmanship employed. In the Islip or Jesus chapel at Westminster Abbey there is a now mutilated image of Christ and on the upper storey of this chapel is a wall painting depicting several

20 Chantry-tomb of Giles de Bridport, Salisbury Cathedral

21 Ramryge chapel, St Albans Abbey

kings, possibly including Edward the Confessor. The theme of many chapel wall paintings was the death and Resurrection of Christ, which linked in with the salvific nature of the mass performed in their spaces. The chapel of Prior Sylke (*c.*1502), tucked away in the north-east corner of the north transept at Exeter Cathedral, contains a wall painting of the Resurrection on the wall of the upper chamber. In the Beauchamp chapel at Tewkesbury Abbey, a particularly fine fifteenth-century painting of Christ's Passion adorns the wall above the site of the chapel altar.

Some chantry chapels represented current trends in architectural style and embellishment. The chapel of Margaret Countess of Richmond at Westminster Abbey, for example, is one of the earliest examples of Renaissance architecture in the country. In the south choir at Ely the chapel of Bishop West (1515-1534) has highly decorated panelled walls that exhibit evidence of the influence of Renaissance design. Italian ornamentation is especially noticeable in the brackets of some of the niches and around the door, where there is a figure in Renaissance costume. Inside, the transitional vault synthesises Gothic fan tracery with a Renaissance panelled ceiling that features moulded ribs with pendant bosses and panels painted with arabesques and figures of cherubs. The cage chantry of Bishop Gardiner (1531-1555) at Winchester is almost entirely Renaissance in its design (*colour plate 5*). The external fabric, in comparison to the other chantries around it, is almost plain and exhibits very minimal ornamentation. Inside, however, it has a panelled vault and a reredos resembling a classical porticus with domed niche.

The design of a chantry chapel itself could also act as a perpetual aid to memory. The Henry V chapel at Westminster Abbey is emblazoned with sculptured visual reminders of Henry's victories in France. In fact, with its embattled walls and stair turrets, it resembles a military fortification, significantly in the shape of a great 'H' for Henry (*22*). At Durham Cathedral, Bishop Thomas Hatfield (1345-1381) built the bishop's throne over a chantry for his tomb, thus forever asserting his status as bishop. At St David's Cathedral, the chantry of Bishop Henry de Gower formed part of the masonry screen at the east end of the nave (*23*). The chapel is a small vaulted compartment at the south end of the screen and contains the effigy of the bishop. A similar, unidentified example without a tomb may exist at Lincoln Cathedral.

COLLEGES

The fourteenth century witnessed another stage in the foundation of chantry chapels with the widespread appearance of collegiate chapels. These institutions

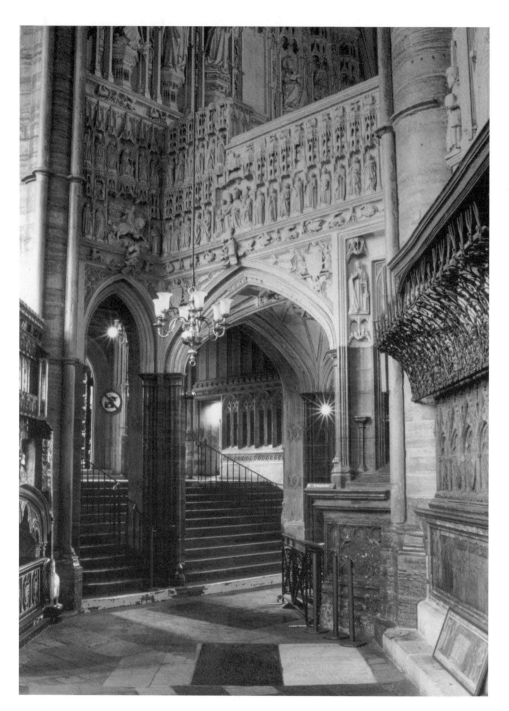

22 Chantry chapel of Henry V, Westminster Abbey (Courtesy of Dean and Chapter of Westminster Abbey)

23 Gower chantry chapel in nave screen, St David's Cathedral

were often solely dedicated to the constant celebration of rounds of masses for very wealthy and influential testators. The medieval collegiate chapel was essentially a chantry institution served by a large collective of priests. Some of the larger foundations were veritable powerhouses of prayer, dedicated to the continuous celebration of divine service for the souls of the dead. Some colleges, such as that at Kilve, were minor foundations with communal dwellings and a chapel served by four or five priests. Others, such as that at Boyton (*24*), Heytesbury and St Mary's, Warwick (*colour plate 7*), were structural, though largely independent components of the parish church. At Crediton, where the collegiate foundation included a communal hall and chapterhouse, there were over 30 canons, vicars, clerks and choir members serving the church. Some colleges were built on the site of battlefields, such as the yet to be discovered but documented chapel founded on the site of one of England's bloodiest battles, the Battle of Towton, fought in 1461. In Shropshire, Battlefield College, the chapel of which still survives as the parish church, was set up to provide intercession for the souls of those slain in the battle of Shrewsbury (1403). Though traditionally ascribed to Henry IV, the college was actually founded mainly by its first master,

24 Collegiate chapel Boyton (looking east). White lines indicate the evidence for earlier features including a south aisle and later chapel buttress (Roffey 2007)

Roger Ive, who was rector of Albright Hussey, the parish in which Battlefield lay. In 1406 he acquired the two-acre site and founded the chapel to celebrate daily masses to be performed by himself and his chaplains for the souls of those who perished in the battle. The site was described by contemporary documents as being surrounded by a ditch and as having entrances to the north and south; within this was the mass burial of many of the dead. Thus a physical link was formed between the dead and their intercessory memorial.

The most impressive collegiate institutions were those initiated by royalty such as those at St George's in Windsor, King's College in Cambridge and Eton. St George's is among the most important and ambitious medieval chantry foundations to have survived in England. The college was founded by Edward III around 1348 and was served by almost 40 clergy. The structure itself is an architectural masterpiece (*colour plate 6*), but it was also of defining importance institutionally in that it set a standard for this type of intercessory institution and was a breeding ground for new and varied forms of religious piety. Rather confusingly, like Edward's own chantry and others such as the nearby Hastings chantry, the college was also later to serve as an umbrella institution for independent chantries founded within its walls. An interesting perspective on the role of these royal institutions has been put forward by Clive Burgess. He has suggested that liturgical developments taking place in these institutions became increasingly identified with wider nationalistic interests. Such a concept, he claims, can be seen in the context of prolonged war with France and the newly found status of the English nation, ever-more investing and engaging in corporate liturgy and 'outstripping the French ... by leading the nation into the paths of righteousness' (Burgess, 2005). Such motives, whether influenced by nationalism or by a desire for religious innovation, may also have filtered down to parish level under the influence of the gentry and mercantile classes.

A series of important royal colleges was founded by Henry VI in the fifteenth century. His foundation in 1440 of 'The King's College of Our Lady of Eton beside Windsor' included a community of secular priests and 70 scholars who received free education (*25*). Henry also founded another similar institution a year later, King's College at Cambridge. At Eton, accommodation for the school consisted of a large dormitory with a schoolroom below. Other buildings included a refectory and accommodation for priests and fellows. However, these important collegiate institutions were not just confined to royalty. Winchester College was founded in 1382 by William of Wykeham, Bishop of Winchester and chancellor to Richard II. It accommodated over 80 scholars and clergy and was the blueprint for Eton and King's College Cambridge. In fact College tradition has it that a 'sod of earth' was transplanted from Winchester College to Eton. The original plan of the Winchester College consisted of three quadrangles which comprised an outer court consisting of the school buildings, a chamber court of accommodation buildings and the cloisters leading to the chapel. The chapel had six bays and a wooden lierne vault. The Thurbern chantry chapel of *c.*1485 lies on the south side (*26*). In the middle of the cloister, and appropriating much of the cloister's open space, is the imposing Fromond chantry chapel of *c.*1420 (*27*). This chapel included a priest's room and later library on the first floor. John Fromond was the college steward; adorning the internal walls of the chapel are carved figures associated with his vocation, including the woodward, the bread butler with trencher and knife and the beer butler with a flagon of ale.

We are fortunate that so many of these impressive monuments have survived the ravages of time. Much of this is thanks to royal connections, though Winchester College uniquely survived and indeed thrived in the period after the Reformation. Others were less fortunate. At Higham Ferrers, the remnants

25 Eton College chapel viewed from Windsor Castle

26 Thurbern chapel and court, Winchester College

27 Fromond chantry chapel, Winchester College

of the former college of Archbishop Henry Chichele now consist of a mere fragment of the original gabled front of the one of the former buildings and some foundations. These are all that survive of the original four ranges of the college buildings. The college was founded in 1422 and was served by a staff of around 20 clergy. Other important colleges of the medieval period include those founded at Arundel, Beverley Minster, Fotheringhay, Tong and Warwick. Technically speaking, many of these 'colleges' bridge the gap between monastery and parish in that they were often a component of the parish church. Thus they demonstrate the difficulty in pigeon-holing certain chantry foundations. We will consider them overall in this chapter but will refer to certain parish-related points later on in the book.

At Fotheringhay, the nave survives from the original fifteenth-century foundation for the royal house of York. The canons at the collegiate church of Beverley were mostly royal officials but were often absent. Vicars and clerics were appointed to carry out their work and were accommodated in the Bedern to the west of the Minster. A college was founded at St Bartholomew's, Tong, by Isabel Pembridge in the early fifteenth century, for her soul and those of her three former husbands. A particularly impressive chantry chapel at Tong is that founded by Sir Henry Vernon to the south of the chancel and was probably completed around 1519. Elements of its decoration were certainly influenced by the Henry VII Chapel at Westminster Abbey. Internally, the chapel is highly decorated and the fan vault with pendants is particularly impressive. The chapel also contains various monuments including the large tomb of Henry Vernon and his wife, replete with effigies and table tomb decorated with mourners. The Beauchamp chapel at the church of St Mary, Warwick (*c.*1440-60) was founded for the influential Richard Beauchamp, Earl of Warwick. In the chapel is the Earl's tomb, consisting of a remarkably life-like and finely crafted gilt bronze recumbent effigy on a Purbeck marble tomb chest (*colour plate 7*). At Arundel, the church of St Nicholas was a parish church and college for the Fitzalan family. The church was originally the church of the dissolved Benedictine priory, but went out of use by 1380 and the chantry college attached to the castle was subsequently moved here. The original iron grille which divides the parochial church from the college chapel still survives. The chapel itself has a Lady Chapel and sacristy to the north and contains several elaborate tombs and chantry chapels of the Fitzalan family including two impressive canopied chapels with masonry altars to the north and south of the altar (*colour plate 8*).

As well as monuments dedicated to intercession and the eventual salvation of the soul, chantry chapels could also represent more worldly and political motivations. One of the largest and most remarkable chapels of the medieval period is that of Henry VII at Westminster (*colour plate 9*). Henry's claim to the throne was tenuous and there were certainly many others still living whose claims were stronger. However, using marriage, astute political manoeuvring and assertions of dynastic continuation, both from ancient Welsh and Lancastrian lineages, he was able to reinvent both himself and his newly founded dynasty. This can no more be in evidence than with his founding of the Henry VII chapel at Westminster, serving both as a royal mausoleum and shrine to the Tudor dynasty. The great detail and fastidiousness that the King put into the design of the chapel is revealed in his will and can be seen in the structure itself. The chapel consisted of a wide nave with side aisles and five radiating chapels, and the decoration originally comprised over 100 saintly and royal figures, including Thomas Becket and Edward the Confessor. The whole superstructure both inside and out, right down to the fixtures and fittings, is peppered with Tudor insignia and connected heraldic devices. To the modern eye the entire monument can appear grossly over the top, but such a view misses the point. The primary motive behind the structure was not overt piety, or even an exhibition of status. Its existence was to establish a physical and highly visual representation of Henry's right to the crown, and thereby to ensure the continuation of his dynasty. Originally it was planned as a shrine to Henry VI for whom Henry had petitioned Rome for canonisation. Henry VII had managed to convince himself of his rightful claim to the throne and in his boundless ambition had pushed aside any ethical or moral considerations inherent in his usurpation.

Construction of the chapel, which replaced an earlier chapel, began in 1503. Several decades later it was described by the antiquarian John Leland as a 'wonder of the entire world'. The chapel has an impressive fan vault embossed with carved pendants, many featuring the familial links of Henry's new-founded dynasty, such as the Beauforts, Nevilles and the ancient Welsh kings. These symbols also adorn the ornate flying buttresses and panels of the chapel's exterior. Behind the altar, enclosed by decorated railings, is the tomb of Henry VII and Elizabeth of York, designed by the Italian Pietro Torrigiano. Ninety-five statues of saints survive, adorning the walls of the chapel. One of these is the female saint Wilgefortis, also known as Uncumber. Her history relates that she was unwilling to comply with an arranged marriage, so she prayed to God to save her from her fate. God's reply was particularly innovative – he caused a beard to grow upon her face, thus putting off her suitor. What is interesting here is that the hagiography attached to the saint symbolises transformation. Perhaps the underlying message here was that one can change under divine influence: if a women can be given the semblance of a man, then why could not a man become a king?

Institutions like the Henry VII's chapel were distinct religious communities in their own right and formed part of a general pattern of collegiate foundations from the fourteenth century onwards. Many of these were singular foundations unattached to any monastic houses and were in fact religious foundations constructed solely for the benefit of individuals or members of the English nobility. In many instances the foundation and endowment of a college attracted the foundation of smaller chantry foundations within its walls. In such cases the college would act as an umbrella organisation for a group of smaller foundations, as at St George's chapel. Another example of this arrangement is the former parochial church of Manchester, which was made collegiate by Thomas de la Warre in 1421. The change in status led to a rebuilding programme that lasted over 80 years. The rebuilding of the church, which included the addition of aisles and side chapels, was seen as opportunity for many wealthy testators to found chantries. The benefits for de la Warre were clear: not only would his service be celebrated at the high altar every day, it would also be greatly enhanced by the round of masses performed by the satellite chantries. Multiple chantry foundation in the collegiate churches of the period was therefore a contributing factor to a wider spiritual network; not only was the spiritual eminence of the primary endowment of the founder enhanced, but testators themselves also benefited from association with institutionalised religious practice that was both concentrated and diverse.

In certain circumstances the college chapel also functioned as the parish church, such as at Boyton, Heytesbury and St Edmund's in Salisbury. The College of St Edmund was founded in 1268 by Bishop Walter de la Wyle, Bishop of Salisbury. The college was actually named in honour of Edmund Rich, Archbishop of Canterbury and one-time treasurer of Salisbury Cathedral, who was canonised in 1248. At this time, Salisbury was a rapidly growing town and the college was partly founded to serve as a parish church. It was endowed with 13 priests who lived in halls, probably to the east of the church. The priests were also expected to take part in some of the major cathedral processions, as well as to have some involvement in the newly founded cathedral school.

HOSPITALS AND ALMSHOUSES

Chantry chapels could also be found in medieval hospitals. In many cases the hospitals were part of chantry endowments, such as Fyfield hospital, which was originally founded in conjunction with a chantry in Fyfield parish church in 1442. The fifteenth-century White Hart Inn that survives in the town was possibly once the chantry priest's lodgings. In 1330, Henry, Earl of Lancaster, established St Mary's hospital at Leicester for a warden, four chaplains, 50 poor and infirm folk, and five women attendants. Around 1355, his son Henry established a chantry college linked to the hospital. As a result, the number of poor people increased to 100. The regulations decreed that a penny a day was set aside for the maintenance of the poor. At the hospital in Stow, additional clergy were provided by chantry endowments. The foundation of a chantry provided the community with financial help, but in return it was often stipulated that the founder should receive their prayers and observances. In 1422, John Barton gave 200 marks and some annual rents to the master and brethren of the hospital of St Thomas of Acon in London for their assistance. In return they had to provide a perpetual chantry priest to pray for his soul and those of his family. At Childrey, the dole (poor payment) to the almshouse men was administered by the priest of William Fettiplace's chantry (*c.*1526).

Medieval hospitals were diverse institutions. Far from being the medical institutions we have today, they often operated more like hostels catering for certain social groups such as the poor, the blind and people afflicted with leprosy. In fact, most leper houses depended on pious endowments for their survival, such as that of Aymer de Valence (*c.*1322), attached to the leper hospital at Gravesend. As such, they often offered the founders not just the opportunity to focus benefactions on the needy elements of society (thus applying one of

28 Almshouses, Ewelme

the Seven Corporal Works of Mercy), but also supplied them with a ready-made and obliging community. At Cirencester, a hospital and chantry were founded by Henry I to house weary travellers as well as the destitute. Many of the hospital inmates were required to wear the livery of their most generous benefactors to demonstrate their loyal affiliation to their master's memory. At Leicester, the warden and chaplains wore habits marked with a white crescent and star. At Ewelme, the brethren of the almshouse were to attend the offices in the founders' chapel and to pray at their tombs (*28*). Any latecomers were subsequently fined from their already meagre pittances. The cloistered accommodation of the brethren still survives intact today, as do elements of the associated school. As at Ewelme, founders' chapels could be attached to churches. At St Mary Spital in London, for example, the wealthy mercer William Eynsham founded his chantry above the hospital's charnel house. A unique survival is that of the Poyntz chapel, founded by Robert Poyntz around 1520 on the south side of the sanctuary at St Mark's hospital in Bristol. The chapel is highly embellished, with Spanish floor tiles and a fan-vaulted ceiling displaying the arms of Henry VIII and Katherine of Aragon and of Poyntz and Woodville.

The monastic and collegiate institutions were remarkable for their time. The colleges in particular were institutions dedicated to intercession, but were also monuments of status, power and prestige. The ideal behind the foundation of these colleges and chapels, whether influenced by nationalism, prestige or by a desire for religious innovation, may have filtered down to parish level under the influence of the gentry and mercantile classes and formed a catalyst for the foundation of chantries in the parish church, a subject to which we will now turn.

CHAPTER 6

THE FORM AND FABRIC
OF CHANTRY CHAPELS
IN THE PARISH

INTRODUCTION

The chantry chapels of the greater religious houses of the medieval period
were particularly versatile, but those founded in the parishes were perhaps even
more so. In theory, as we have seen, all that was required for the foundation of
a chantry was a defined altar and a priest. Although the primary recipient of
chantry foundation in the parish was the parish church, chantries could also be
founded within a range of suitable structures including castles, private houses,
bridges and city gatehouses. Indeed one could argue that it was because of its
versatility that chantry foundation was one of the most widespread and popular
religious movements in the late medieval period. We will now examine some of
these various categories of parish foundation.

BRIDGES, WALLS, GATES AND HOUSES

Many bridges of the medieval period had chapels built upon them. The foundation
of a chantry within a bridge chapel enabled benefactors to attract the prayers
and observations of a host of people entering and leaving the towns on these
often busy thoroughfares. For the community they often provided a convenient
place for divine service and the liturgical celebrations in such foundations were
arranged accordingly. For example, the mass performed in the chapel on the
Fosse Bridge in York had formerly been timed from 11 o'clock to noon, but was
altered on the advice of the parishioners to an earlier time, to cater for travellers

entering and leaving the city. The chantry certificate of 1546 for the chapel on Wakefield Bridge indicated that the chapel also had an auxiliary use as a place where divine service could be held for the sick in times of plague, so that the rest of the parishioners could continue to use their parish churches without fear of infection. As an added attraction, some bridge chapels, such as that at Caversham, also held relics. In some cases chapels were also used by hermits, such as that on 'New Bridge' on the River Thames. Here the hermit was licensed to collect tolls for bridge maintenance. In Derby a cell was constructed in the fourteenth century for an anchoress (a religious recluse). It later became a hermit's dwelling and by the fifteenth century there was a company of the 'Sisters of Our Lady and Child of the Bridge'. Bridge chapels were frequently built on an extended pier on one side of the bridge, as in the case of the surviving chapel at Wakefield. Occasionally chapels may have spanned the entire width of the bridge; in the mid-sixteenth century the antiquarian John Leland refers to a timber chapel spanning the bridge at Droitwich. In the eighteenth century the historian Nash adds that the public road with horses and carts passed through the chapel, the congregation sitting on one side of the road, the priest on the other. The chapel was pulled down in this century, but another timber chapel was constructed on the bridge at Bewdley in the same county.

Today only a handful of these chapels survive and all of these have been reorganised and restored to varying extents. The surviving chapels include those on the bridges at Wakefield (*colour plate 10*), Rotherham, St Ives and Bradford-on-Avon; these are discussed in more detail below. Many other examples are known from documentary sources. For example, at Exeter the 'chaplain of the bridge' appears in a document of 1196, and this may be the 'chapel of St Edmund' on the Exe Bridge recorded some 20 years later. In 1200, a bridge chapel was founded on London Bridge in honour of St Thomas of Canterbury. Contemporary illustrations show that the chapel was situated on the downstream side of the bridge and extended out onto the river. The chapel attracted several chantry foundations throughout the thirteenth and fourteenth centuries and the numerous priests were housed in their own accommodation at Bridge House. The chapel collapsed some time before 1396 and was replaced by a new two-storey chapel with a five-sided apse to the east. By 1541 only one priest served St Thomas's chapel, and on the suppression of the chantries the building was converted to a dwelling and grocer's shop before being finally demolished in 1553.

Other recorded bridge chapels include that at High Bridge, Lincoln, the chapel of the Assumption on Bristol Bridge and the chapel that once stood on the north end of Trent Bridge, Nottingham. At Salisbury, St John's chapel occupied a small midstream island east of Harnham Bridge. In 1392 the Guild of St Mary in Stamford was granted a licence to endow a chantry in the chapel of St Mary-at-the-Bridge and at Coventry a chapel was built for the Fraternity of St George on the bridge over the River Sherbourne in the early fifteenth century. Often, the incumbents of bridge chapels had responsibilities toward the fabric and operation of their bridges. At Lechlade, for example, the priest of the bridge chapel had specific responsibilities towards its repair. At Wallingford, the Mary Grace chapel was built into an archway at the town end of the bridge and accommodated priests whose duty it was to collect benefactions for its upkeep.

The earliest and finest of the surviving examples of bridge chapels is the chantry chapel of St Mary the Virgin on the bridge over the River Calder at Wakefield (*29*), though its presence is slightly at odds with its modern run-down setting. It is situated south of the city and was built between 1342 and 1356, the date when the chapel was licensed. The west front of the chapel was divided into five panels and contained depictions of the annunciation, nativity, resurrection, ascension and the coronation of the Virgin. Beneath the depictions are five arches, three containing doorways and the other two adorned with tracery. In the north-east corner of the building is a winding staircase leading

29 Bridge chapel, Wakefield

to the roof and bell tower; the staircase also descends to a small crypt. At St Ives the bridge chapel was built around 1415 and consisted of a small stone chapel built out from the third pier from the town end, with a semi-hexagonal apse. The bridge chapel at Rotherham, restored in 1924, is of two bays, with a tunnel-vaulted crypt below. The chapel is referred to in the will of the master of the town grammar school and was begun around 1483. It is similar to the Wakefield chapel but more limited in its decoration. The chapel on the bridge at Bradford-on-Avon, though surviving in part, was almost completely rebuilt in the seventeenth century. There is also some documentary evidence indicating that a number of chapels were located close to river crossings and causeways. Examples are documented on the Northdyke causeway at Stickney and Holland Bridge causeway in Lincolnshire. Whether or not these chapels served specifically as chantries is unknown.

Other practical and profitable locations for chapels were town walls, bastions and gatehouses. Such locations allowed the chapels to attract passing custom, as in the case of those located on bridges. For example, in the early fourteenth century, the Trinitarian Friars in Oxford founded a chantry in the chapel of the Holy Trinity by the east gate of the city precisely to 'catch' the prayers for their deceased brethren and benefactors. One of the earliest gate chapels, dating to the late tenth century, was that of St Michael, located above the east gate in Winchester. Chapels over town gates were numerous. In Southampton, a chapel dedicated to St Mary stood over the east gate and chapels stood over the east and west gates at Warwick. St James' chapel over the west gate was founded as a chantry chapel for the Guild of St George the Martyr by the Earl of Warwick in the 1380s (*30*). A tower was added to the west side of the single-room chapel in the fifteenth century. The chantry chapel of St John the Baptist in Wakefield stood on the east side of the road from Wakefield to Leeds, a few hundred metres from the town gate. The chapel was probably founded some time in the late thirteenth century and was rebuilt at some point around the second decade of the fourteenth century, when a large bell tower, or campanile, was added. An anchorite/anchoress also served the chapel and his or her cell was situated on the south side of the chapel.

A unique example of a gatehouse chapel is that of Langport. The rather unusual looking fifteenth-century guild chapel of St Mary comprises a gabled building above a barrel-vaulted archway spanning the road close to the east gate of the medieval town. An external stairway gave access to the chapel, whilst a doorway in the south wall led to a room on the south side at a lower level. Like the Winchester example, the original chapel may have had earlier origins. Excavations in the 1990s for a new footpath to the north of the chapel revealed that it was situated next to the Anglo-Saxon defensive bank constructed around

30 Chantry chapel of St James over the medieval west gate, Warwick

the town in the ninth century. Chapels could also be found above castle or cathedral gates. For example, at Cambridge there was a chapel over the barbican gate of the castle, whilst at Salisbury and York chapels formerly stood above gates into the cathedrals' precincts.

Many well-appointed medieval houses had private chapels. These gave wealthy members of the laity an opportunity to fashion and control their religious practice directly, in a more domestic environment. Naturally, many of these chapels were primarily for the use of the living. However, they were undoubtedly also a potential context for intercession on the behalf of the souls of the deceased householders or members of the family. Household chapels could be located in a variety of places within the house and grounds. At Place Court in Colaton Raleigh, the small fourteenth-century chapel, with connected chamber, was located above the porch of the house. At Lypiatt Park, Bisley-with-Lypiatt, a two-cell chapel with a large bellcote is located in the corner of the courtyard of a sixteenth-century manor house. The masonry-built Dane Chantry in Petham was attached to the southern end of the half-timbered manor house. An account of the manor house at Chingford in 1265 tells us a little about the original arrangement of such buildings, recording that 'there is a decent chapel covered with tiles, a portable altar and a small cross …'. We are also informed that a chamber 'suitable for a clergyman' was within the inner gate.

One unique survival is the chantry recorded in Bridport. Now a private house, the structure was built not long after Bridport received its Town Charter in 1253 and may have originally operated as a toll house. However, by 1362, the town bailiffs leased the building to Robert Bemynstre, a local lawyer. A chantry was endowed on the first floor of the building, possibly dedicated to St Katherine and the Virgin Mary. The building was also used as accommodation for a priest, Richard Stratton, who was employed to celebrate masses for the souls of Bemynstre's family and the burgesses of Bridport and their successors. Today, the first floor consists of a landing and a main bedroom, which contains a fourteenth-century fireplace and garderobe. From this, an archway gave access to a chamber above the porch. This space still has a piscina, and it was here that the chantry mass was celebrated.

Despite the variety of locations that were actually used, the most preferable option for the foundation of a chantry chapel was the parish church. As we have seen, some parish churches were close to manor houses, many of these having their origins in the privately founded churches of the late Anglo-Saxon period. The parish church offered a more intimate and community-based context for intercessory practice. Thus individual memory was publicly celebrated, drawing in the valuable prayers of the whole parish.

THE PARISH CHURCH

Compared with monastic and cathedral examples, the parish church chantry chapel has until recently received relatively little attention. However, when compared with the greater religious houses, it is from the parish church examples that we can gain a better insight into religious practice as experienced by the majority of medieval society, as well as the crucial role performed by the chantry within it. Most former parish chantry chapels have, however, vanished. Where they do survive, they are often surplus to requirements and have been adapted to the changing needs and functional necessities of a modern parish church. That being said, some still remain in part and some remarkable and singular examples do survive, particularly in the parish churches of East Anglia and the south-west of England, where the communities had grown rich on the wool trade. These often present particularly outstanding examples. In other instances, chantry chapels can be reconstructed by combining spatial and archaeological evidence with documentary sources. The surviving physical remains of chantry foundations, though fragmentary in many cases, demonstrate a certain diversity of design. As such, they often reflect both the individual considerations behind their design and their relationship with the rest of church space.

One of the simplest forms of memorial practice was a request for a light to burn in the church on certain occasions. In 1398 John Watford, rector of the church of Snergate, requested that five wax candles be burnt around his grave and before an image of the Virgin Mary. In some churches niches were provided for commemorative lights such as the so-called 'poor man's light' in the porch of Aldsworth church. Here a small niche, containing a cresset, was cut through the east wall of the porch and allowed the laity to place a candle whilst viewing the altar in the north aisle and the chancel, thus forging a ritual link between the candle and the masses performed at the respective altars. An unusual example of a chantry 'chapel' was the diminutive Barnard chapel in St Mary's, Luton. This chapel is arguably one of the smallest in the country and is particularly unique. It comprises a small sunken recess in the south wall of the chancel, the floor being about 35cm below the chancel floor. The chapel was founded by Richard Bedford, vicar of Luton in 1477-92. The small structure has a lierne vault and a separate entrance with lobby. Such monuments indicate how strategies for the afterlife could still be devised despite the limitations of space and finances.

Chantry chapels could also be founded in churchyards, as at Scarborough and possibly at Buckfastleigh. At Bray the chantry chapel of Our Lady that stands in the churchyard was probably built around the same time as the church. At Chew Magna the large earthwork to the north of the church is likely to be the remains of the former churchyard chantry of Our Lady. Though relatively rare compared with monastic examples, some parish churches contained stone-cage chantries. Examples such as the early sixteenth-century Markham and Meyring chapels at Newark were clearly attempts to imitate those found in cathedrals. Both these chapels occupy an important position in the chancel of the church; the earlier Meyring chapel (*31*) is to the north and the Markham chapel is to the south (*colour plate 11*). The Meyring chapel, founded by Thomas Meyring in 1500, is a largely enclosed stone-cage chapel with a stepped eastern entrance and is decorated with shields, image niches and panels inside and out. The Markham chapel, founded by Robert Markham in or around 1505, is decorated with shields and panels, two of which contain depictions of the 'dance of death' (*32*). Both chapels have open arcades through open to the chancel within which tombs may have once resided. At St John the Baptist's in Burford, the small parclosed chapel of St Peter was located against the east respond of the north aisle. It is now 'restored' with wooden screens originally dismantled during the Reformation. However, at its east end there is a fourteenth-century stone canopy

31 Meyring chapel, Newark church

which formed part of a chantry chapel that adjoined the rood-screen. A similar arrangement may have occurred at St Mary's, Chipping Norton, where a guild chapel was founded about 1450 at the altar of St Katherine by the vicar and local wool merchants, who installed two chaplains. This chapel was located in front of the north pillar of the chancel arch, where the carved reredos, with its three canopied niches, still exists (*33*). The chapel probably extended westwards as far as the next pier and was enclosed by timber screens on three sides, perhaps with a decorated canopy above. The Spring chapel at the church of Saints Peter and Paul, Lavenham, was founded by Thomas Spring around 1525. Situated on the north side of the chancel, the chapel is enclosed by a unique wooden canopied parclose which also had small elevation squints inserted into it (*colour plate 12*). A similar example, the Spourne chantry chapel, is situated on the south side of the church (*34*). Another impressive example is that of the 'Garstang' chapel in the south aisle at Cirencester. In all probability, there were many more of these wooden chapels in the medieval parish churches. However, it is likely that being made of wood, their removal and destruction was comparatively easy for the iconoclasts of the Reformation.

1 Wharram Percy church. Earlier phases of the church are marked out in the foreground

2 Medieval painting of the 'Doom', or Day of Judgment, South Leigh church

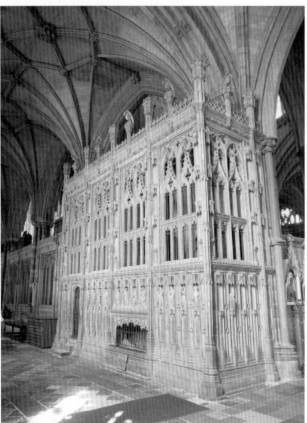

Above: 3 The Harys chapel
(*c.*1520), Christchurch Priory

Left: 4 Chantry chapel
of Bishop Fox (1500-28),
Winchester Cathedral

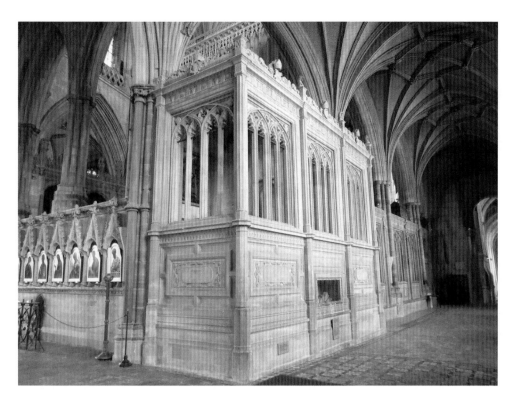

5 Chantry chapel of Bishop Gardiner (1531-55), Winchester Cathedral

6 St George's chapel, Windsor

7 Fifteenth-century Beauchamp chapel, St Mary's, Warwick

Right: 8 Fitzalan chapel and tomb of Thomas and Beatrix Fitzalan (*c.*1415), Arundel

Below: 9 Henry VII chapel, Westminster Abbey (Dean and Chapter of Westminster Abbey)

10 Bridge chapel, Wakefield

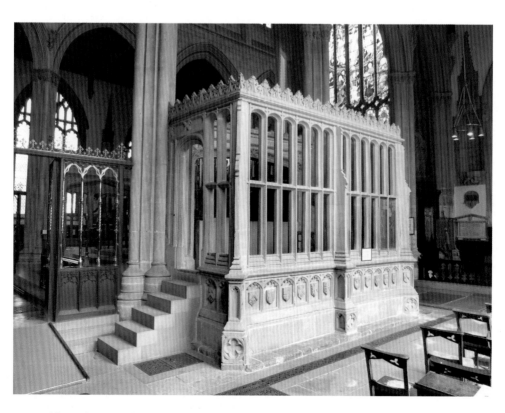

11 Markham chapel (c.1505), Newark church

12 Spring chapel (*c.*1525), Lavenham church

13 South wall of Clopton chapel, Long Melford, showing decorative panels, niches and painted inscriptions (*c.*1490s)

14 Greenway chantry chapel, Tiverton church (*c.*1517)

15 Elaborately decorated east gable of Beauchamp chapel, Devizes. Note large central niche once holding an image of the Virgin Mary

16 Elaborate western façade of the fourteenth-century chapel at Gaddesby church

17 Sixteenth-century Babbington monument and chantry chapel as seen from the chancel at Kingston-on-Soar parish church

18 Fan vault, Wilcote chantry chapel, North Leigh (*c.*1440)

Above: 19 Interior of St John's chapel, Ewelme

Left: 20 Sixteenth-century Christ on the Lily Cross and rebus for John Leigh ('le Leigh' or 'Leigh Leigh') in Leigh chapel, Godshill (Roffey 2007)

Above: 21 Detail of Lydgate's verses, Clopton chantry chapel, Long Melford church

Right: 22 Chantries of Bishop Beaufort (1405–1447), left, and Wayneflete (1447–86), right, crowd around the former site of St Swithun's shrine, Winchester Cathedral

23 The chantry chapel of Margaret Countess of Salisbury (d.1541) last direct descendant of the Plantagenets, next to the high altar, Christchurch Priory

24 De la Warr chantry chapel, Boxgrove Priory

Above: 25 'Enraptured in timeless adoration'. Detail of gilt-bronze effigy of Richard Beauchamp (d.1439), St Mary's, Warwick

Right: 26 Tomb of Lady Eleanor Percy (*c.*1365), Beverley Minster

27 Fourteenth-century Easter sepulchre and tomb, Lincoln Cathedral

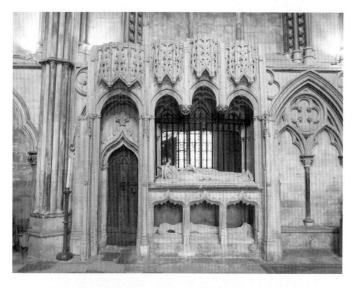

28 Chantry chapel and transi-tomb of Bishop Fleming (*c.*1425), Lincoln Cathedral

29 Post-Reformation pews in the former chantry chapel, Rycote

32 Depiction
of 'Dance of
Death' on panel
of Markham
chapel, Newark

33 Medieval reredos marking former location of chantry chapel at Chipping Norton church

Most parish churches had at least one chantry foundation and many had purpose-built chapels, particularly in the wealthier rural areas and in the towns. The Church of Holy Trinity, Kendal, for example, had several chantries at the east end of the chancel south aisle. One of these was the Parr chapel, dating to the fourteenth century and probably founded by the Parr family, who inhabited Kendal Castle in the early part of that century. To the west of the Parr chapel was St Mary's chantry, founded in 1321. Two other chapels were located in the chancel aisles: the Strickland Chapel to the south and the Beckett or Chambre chapel to the north. The Bellingham chapel, of the late fifteenth or early sixteenth century, was founded in the north outer aisle of the chancel.

34 Spourne chapel, Lavenham church

Significantly, the foundation of a chantry chapel often provided an extension to church space. At Old Basing, the north and south Paulet chapels each had internal spaces larger than that of the chancel which they flanked (*35*). In other cases the foundation of a chantry necessitated the construction of an aisle, often beside the chancel or flanking the nave, like the Birde and Horton chantries established in the north aisle at Holy Trinity, Bradford-on-Avon, in the early sixteenth century. At St Andrew's in Cullompton, an outer south aisle was built by John Lane, a local wool merchant, in 1525-6 (d.1528), highly embellished with his personal motifs, symbols of his trade and religious imagery (*36*). Other chantry foundations provided transepts, as at Bridgwater, and side chapels, such at the Greenway chapel in Tiverton (*colour plate 14*).

Many parish church chantry priests were accommodated in dwellings close to the church, such as the remarkable fifteenth-century chantry priest's house surviving at Farleigh Hungerford. In other cases accommodation may have been inside the church itself. At St Alphege's, Solihull, a rib-vaulted undercroft below the chantry chapel provided accommodation for the priest. The chantry of Haliwell (or Holy Well) was founded in 1277 by William de Odingsells and in

35 Old Basing church showing north and south chancel chapels

36 The Lane aisle, Cullompton church

1438 an endowment by Thomas Greswold was added. The chapel, which is on the north-east side of the chancel, has a unique two-storey arrangement. Little has changed since 1277 when this was possibly the chantry priest's chamber, with his chapel above. Shutter hinges still exist in the jambs of the windows and in the west wall is a fireplace. Unusually, the original chapel altar still survives. At All Saints, East Horndon, there is an unusual brick-built two-storey shallow south transept of the late fifteenth century, possibly associated with the Tyrell family. Inside, a south gallery led to a priest's room with a fireplace. A similar arrangement can be found at Montacute church in Somerset, where a small stairway from the chapel led to what was probably a former priest's room above the porch.

Some chantry chapels were composite structures, featuring a porch, lobby and sometimes a series of chapels. In the Beauchamp chapels at Bromham and Devizes, there were small 'lobbies' attached to the chapel with stone seating along the walls. At St Mary's in Warwick, the small chapel situated between the church chancel and the Beauchamp chapel has a small seating area with original wooden benches (37). The Clopton 'chapel' at Long Melford (c.1490s) was also a composite chapel, comprising a western chapel with a chantry chapel to the

37 Wooden pews, St Mary's Warwick

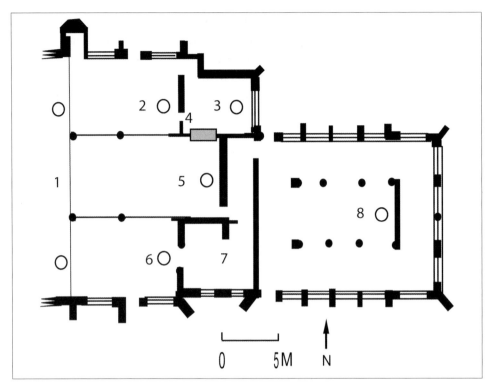

38 Plan of east end of Long Melford parish church showing location of Clopton chapels:
1) rood screen and altars 2) Clopton chapel 3) Clopton chantry chapel 4) squint and tomb/
Easter sepulchre 5) high altar 6) Martin chapel 7) Choir vestry and passage 8) Lady chapel

east, approached by a tiny vestibule or priest's room with panelled ceiling and
fireplace. The chapel and chantry are one component of a series of distinct ritual
areas at the east end of the church that included south chapels, a choir vestry, a
priest's passage and, unusually for a parish church, a separate Lady chapel (*38*).
The chantry chapel itself is a particularly outstanding example (*colour plate 13*).

In some cases, the foundation of chantry chapels would contribute to the
rebuilding of other parts of the church. For example, in the fifteenth century,
Thomas Spring of Lavenham provided money for the building of a lavishly
decorated upper storey to the west tower, as well as for the foundation and
construction of his chantry chapel. Often pious benefactors associated themselves
with church rebuilding programmes, which not only acted as an example
of their pious charity and local prestige, but also presented an architectural
canvas for the display of personal motifs. At St Ethelbert's, Hessett, a dedicatory
inscription on the two-storey vestry requested prayers for the souls of John and
Katherine Hoo, who paid for work on the chancel and aisles. The fifteenth-

century clerestory at St Mary's, Grundisburgh, was decorated with flushwork monograms that punctuated the windows. These included the badge of St Edmund, letters spelling out AVE and possibly the monograms of Thomas and Anne Tudenham, who paid for the work. However, we should be aware that the motives behind such endowments were not necessarily altruistic. For example the newly extended tower at Grundisbergh highlighted the largesse and prestige of its donors as well as benefiting the church.

Some parish church chantry chapels may have been associated with anchorite cells. At Compton parish church a small stairway containing a small cubicle and a prayer desk, led from the chancel of the parish church to a chapel situated directly above. It is likely that the cubicle formed part of a now lost anchorite cell. Commonly, as at Compton, anchorite cells were built close to chancels, but there is evidence to suggest that at Devizes, and possibly Britford, anchorite cells were built against chantry chapels.

The foundation of a chantry chapel could also, as part of its conditions, provide for the construction of a porch, which was normally spatially associated with the chapel itself, such as at Cullompton and Tiverton. The elaborate north porch at Yaxley was probably erected by the local Yaxley family in the fifteenth century. The vaulted ceiling has bosses, now defaced, depicting the annunciation and the four evangelists. Porches could also be places of burial; the will of John Yaxley in 1459 requested burial in the porch and for 'the rest of the porch to be paved at my cost'. The floor slabs, formerly bearing brasses to John and his son Richard (d.1503), were in the porch until the general 'restoration' of the mid-eighteenth century. Porches could be used for a variety of communal activities such as baptisms, weddings and funerals, and therefore presented a valuable opportunity for memorial practice. The building of porches also allowed benefactors to promote themselves in a highly visual context, and these structures were therefore often adorned with personal devices and motifs. At Cullompton church, a porch was constructed as part of a chantry foundation by John Lane (*c.*1525). The porch formed the west bay of the inner south aisle and an inscription commemorating Lane runs at low level along the west wall of the aisle so that it could be viewed by all those entering the church (*39*). Perhaps one of the best examples of this arrangement can be seen in the Greenway Chapel of St Peter's in Tiverton. The south porch and chapel, built by the merchant and ship-owner John Greenway in 1517, are decorated with niches and friezes of ships that possibly refer to Greenway's own vessels, which operated out of Dartmouth (*40; colour plate 14*). At St Mary's, Grundisburgh, a chantry chapel was constructed at the east end of the south aisle by Thomas Wale on the eve of the Reformation in 1527. A dedicatory inscription runs below the battlements and requests prayers for Wale's soul and that of his wife. The reliefs, however, depict

39 Commemoration script to John Lane, Cullompton church

40 Detail of external decoration of Greenway chapel, Tiverton, showing ships and maritime symbols of founder's trade including heraldic shields in the form of sails symbols of Wale's economic status and show both his merchant mark and the shield of the Salt Merchants' Company, of which he was a member. The Savage chapel, at St Michael's, Macclesfield, is a large chapel flanking the south aisle built by Thomas Savage, Archbishop of York (1501-1507). The two-bay chapel has a highly decorated three-storey porch to the west with canopied niches and an oriel window. The porch is adorned with the shields of Rochester, London and York, the places where Thomas Savage was bishop before becoming the Archbishop of York. At Montacute, the chapel was connected to the church porch by a narrow lobby. At Wedmore, the guild chapel was inserted between the south transept and the porch. Here, however, a separate entrance leads from the porch into the chapel and two internal windows provided a view into the chapel. In both these latter examples, there was a conscious desire to make the chapels accessible from communal areas. At Bridgwater, the reconstruction of the north aisle, some time around 1400 for the foundation of two chantry chapels, also made provision for a large two-storey porch.

Chantry chapels were often outstanding additions to parish church space, introducing new forms of architectural innovation and display. In some cases, as at Tiverton, chapels architecturally outclassed the church itself. However, in other instances the foundation and construction of chantry chapels was sensitive to the overall aesthetic needs of the church fabric. For example, the south transept chapel of Our Lady of the Bower at Bishops Cannings was aligned south-east and therefore away from the body of the church. This arrangement limited the obstruction of light into the chancel. Sometimes the construction of a chapel was part of a larger building campaign. At Bishops Cannings and nearby All Cannings, the south chapels were constructed at the same time as the south transept. At Crewkerne and Ilminster, the chapels were integral components of the newly-constructed transepts (*41*). Similarly, at Lacock, the north chapel was constructed at the same time as the chancel was rebuilt. These examples may suggest planning on the part of the clergy or local laity to provide extra church space.

The contribution of chantry chapel foundation to the overall layout and expansion of parish churches is particularly noticeable in the wealthier towns of the period. The church of St John the Baptist in Cirencester had a remarkable arrangement of chapels which were clustered around the church. These included the north chancel chapel of St Catherine, the south chancel chapel of St John the Baptist and the north Lady Chapel, extended in the mid-fifteenth century. There was also the large four-bay chapel of the Holy Trinity on the north side of the nave and the smaller Garstang chapel of *c.*1440 in the south-east corner of the nave. St Mary's in Scarborough had four chapels which, unusually, were built side-by-side at right angles to the south aisle and extended from the transept to the porch. All the chapels were founded within a few years of each other.

41 Transept chapel, Crewkerne, looking south-west

In 1380 the chapel of St James was constructed to the east of the church next to the south transept. It was licensed to pray for the soul of Robert Galon – a wealthy burgher of Scarborough who endowed it with the sum of six pounds per annum. The chapel of St Nicholas, to the west of this, was licensed and probably completed in 1390 as a chantry for Agnes Burn. A third chapel, founded by William de Rillington, was dedicated to St Stephen and was licensed in 1381. The fourth and westernmost chapel was dedicated to Our Lord Jesus Christ, the Blessed Virgin Mary and All Saints. Its license dates from 1390, but its foundation did not take place until 1397. The foundation declared its establishment for the souls of Emily, Edwin and Reginald Mylner. There was also a chapel of St Mary Magdalene in the churchyard. In other instances, such as St Bride's on Fleet Street in London and Holy Trinity in Coventry, almost half of the internal space was occupied by chantry and guild foundations. Thus many of the highly influential urban merchant classes were represented by corporate foundation of chantries and guilds within their respective churches.

PARISH GUILDS

Many chantries took the form of Guild chapels. Guilds and fraternities played an important role in medieval religion, providing specific groups of the laity with a focus for orthodox piety through devotional practices and group ceremonial. Many of these guilds provided chapels for the exclusive use of members; in essence, their chapels functioned as collective chantry chapels, except generally for a large group of people. Many medieval trades and crafts were represented by guilds and were thus hugely influential in local economy and politics. In many cases the form, fabric and location of guild chapels reflected their influence and prestige in the towns and parishes. At Coventry, three of the largest chapels in the church belonged to the important mercers', tanners' and butchers' guilds. The Church of Holy Trinity in Hull is one of the largest parish churches in the country and was the location for many influential guilds. The north chancel chapel was founded in 1526-7 and built by Richard Marler, a Coventry merchant. The ceiling is finely carved, the west bay in particular, which has a vine scroll pattern and Marler's merchant's mark. In the south transept was the 'Jesus chapel' dating from around 1478. There was originally a public passageway under the transept. A priest's house was also built next to the south wall and referred to as 'Jesus Hall'. North of the nave and east of the porch was the chapel of St Thomas the Martyr, originally founded in 1296. Other chapels included the Tanners' chapel at the west end of the south aisle, the Butchers' chapel in the chancel south aisle and the Lady and Trinity chapels toward the north and south of the sanctuary respectively. At St Mary's in Chipping Norton, the Trinity guild chapel was founded about 1450 at the altar of St Katherine by the vicar and four wool merchants, who installed two chaplains. As noted, this chapel may have been located in front of the north pillar of the chancel arch, where a carved reredos exists.

Although the parish churches were the more popular and practical choice of guild location, some cathedrals and colleges also contained them. For example at Beverley Minster, the tilers' and dyers' guilds maintained a light before the crucifix inside the north door of the Minster, whilst the porters and goldsmiths were associated with the altar of St Christopher in the nave. The cooks were associated with the chapel of St Catherine and the tailors with the altar of St Andrew. The butchers also maintained an annual mass in the church of the Grey Friars. However, it appears that the parish church of St Mary was a particularly popular location for the town guilds, testament to the prestige of the town's commercial classes. Of particular note is the guild chapel of St Michael, to the north of the chancel. Built around 1330, it is an outstanding example of contemporary architectural style. The chapel, which contains a magnificent vaulted ceiling and traceried windows, has a small sacristy to the north and priest's rooms above. Some guild chapels were entirely separate from the church, such as the chapel at Holy Trinity, Buckfastleigh, the remains of which still stand in the churchyard. At Pulham, a local guild was formed of hatters and hurers (cappers) who were successful enough to build a chapel dedicated to

St James the Lesser (the patron saint of hatters and milliners). The foundation was originally attached to the church, but was moved to the centre of the village in the early fifteenth century. Part of the building survives and is incorporated into the village school. Many guild and fraternities also had social responsibilities. For example, the King Edward VI grammar school at Stratford-on-Avon in Warwickshire was originally the site of a religious fraternity dedicated to the Holy Cross in the mid-thirteenth century. It provided a hospital and almshouses in the town, held regular feasts and also had a small school to teach members' sons Latin grammar.

PARISH CHANTRY CHAPELS: ART AND ARCHITECTURE

Like their monastic counterparts, many parish chantry chapels boasted a high standard of architectural design. Many examples, such as the chapels at Bromham, Devizes and Tiverton, were peppered with artistic detail and were clearly designed to make a visual statement (*42; colour plate 15*). In some cases, the external elevations of chapels were embellished with secular and religious symbols, often denoting status, familial affiliations and religious sensibilities. As such, the external fabric potentially represented a sort of 'canvas' upon which

42 Architectural detail on the Beauchamp chapel, Bromham

architectural 'messages' could be inscribed. This was particularly relevant where the use of overt decoration and symbolism could be used to draw attention to such structures as monuments associated with individuals desiring a statement or context for intercessory practice. As noted, the three-storey porch associated with the Savage chapel at Macclesfield featured the shields of Rochester, London and York. At Old Basing, the north external elevation of the north chapel was embellished with label stops containing the emblems of the Paulet founders and at least seven other connected families. Such devices could be seen as intercessory markers and/or statements of the family's religious fervour for personal or social gain. By contrast, at Devizes and Bromham, the external elevations of the south chapels are adorned with heraldic symbols, canopied niches and angels grasping shields depicting the instruments of the passion, designed to attract attention and prayers from people outside the chapel. Here the founders are directly linked to intercessory motifs. The Berkeley chapel at St Mary's in Berkeley has a lierne vault with carved bosses depicting the annunciation and assumption of the Blessed Virgin, the Holy Trinity and Christ in glory. There are also symbols of the four evangelists and badges of the Berkeley family. Externally, the chapel's parapet has carved enrichments of strawberry leaves and figures of angels holding shields. At St Andrew's in Cullompton an inscription commemorating John Lane (*c*.1525) runs at low level along the west wall of the aisle he built (*39*). At St Luke's, Gaddesby, the impressive three-bay south aisle chapel stands out from the rest of the church by the superior quality of its stonework and the elaborately decorated exterior. The chapel is of the mid-fourteenth century and has a highly decorated western façade with a motif of a large window in the form of a triangle which encloses three cusped quadrangles. There is also a row of narrow blank gables accompanying three niches, a central doorway and decorated battlements. The carved stone cornice contains a variety of interesting and imaginative subjects, such as human and animal heads, chickens and hens and mermaids (*colour plate 16*).

Highly decorated and unusual windows also emphasised the status of many chantry chapels and by association the prestige of their founders. For example, the Bellingham chapel at Kendal contained a clerestory with an unusual eastern rose window, whilst the west wall of the south chapel at Boyton has a remarkable fourteenth-century circular tracery window of substantial size (*24*). Such additions are not only unique to the church but are also generally outstanding architectural features throughout the region. At St Bartholomew's in Ducklington, the north aisle, possibly the chapel of the Dyve family from the thirteenth and fourteenth centuries, was decorated with elaborate flowing tracery on the windows; the tracery of the east window had a continuous string course of ballflowers and motifs of the coronation of the Virgin (which was linked with stained glass).

There are also some disfigured sculptures depicting the life of Mary. The aisle contains two ogee-recesses decorated with vines and grapes which issue from a crouched figure at the point where the canopies meet, possibly representing the biblical Jesse. In the Lane aisle at Cullompton the slim internal buttresses are beautifully carved with various personal and religious symbols (*43*). The interior of the Sharrington chapel at Lacock was decorated with sculptured and painted images of plants and flowers and small animals that dangled and crawled around its arches, piers and shafts. Such decoration may have promoted a sort of natural forest glade effect to the chapel's interior, and may have sought a particular aesthetic response. Many other chapels contained rich decoration in the form of canopied niches (no doubt once containing beautiful devotional images) sculptures and wall paintings, much of which is now lost.

Because of the individual influence on many chantry chapels they often contained or exhibited more unusual architectural features, such as the 'burial cloister' built onto the outside wall of the south chapel at Bishopstone. Another unusual monument is that to Thomas Babington at St Winifred's in Kingston-on-Soar (*colour plate 17*). The memorial, on the south side of the chancel, is a form of setting for a chantry and/or a now lost tomb. It contains an ornate canopy, probably constructed by Thomas Babington (*c*.1540-47). Possibly not in its original location, it comprises decorated columns with a network of hexagonal panels containing figures and tracery. One row has a depiction of the dance of death, others have saints and images. The capitals are decorated with carvings of babes and tuns (a play on words for 'Babington'). Inside the east wall of the monument is a relief of the Last Judgment (*44*).

The presence of stone vaulting in parish churches is rare, the church of St Mary Redcliffe in Bristol being an outstanding example. However, many chantry chapels were vaulted in stone, often highly decorated and emblazoned with images and secular devices. For example, the masonry vault of the Wilcote chantry in North Leigh is unique to the county (*colour plate 18*). The fan vault in Abbot Lichfield's chapel at Evesham parish church is a particularly impressive example. At Cullompton the vault of the Lane chantry aisle is vaulted with pendants depicting symbols of the Passion, as well as shears and tin, alluding to trade of John Lane who was a prominent wool merchant. In the Spencer chapel in Great Brington, the magnificent fan-vaulted polygonal recessed bay window was clearly influenced by that in the Henry VII chapel at Westminster Abbey and perhaps serves to illustrate the dynastic pretensions of this particular family. Many chapels also had impressive wooden ceilings, such as the panelled and painted ceilings from the south chapel at Ewelme and that from the Rose chapel, Salle. Here the roof bosses on the beam intersections of the ceiling are carved with 'T's and roses to serve as a visual reminder of the founder and recipient of

43 Depictions of saints on internal 'buttresses' of Lane aisle arcade, Cullompton

44 Carved panel featuring the Day of Judgment on the Babington memorial, Kingston-on-Soar church

the masses and prayers enacted within the chapel. Many ceilings were painted, as in the Rose chapel. Evidence for painted ceilings survives for example in the Sharrington chapel, Lacock, and in the Swayne chapel at St Thomas, Salisbury. In the south chancel chapel at St Mary's, Bury St Edmunds, is a remarkable fifteenth-century ceiling inscribed with the legend *Grace me Governe* with illuminated capitals and tiny stars that appear to have mirrored centres.

In many chantry chapels the survival of religious art is limited. Much pre-Reformation art was destroyed, especially imagery and movable or temporary decorations, such as hangings, altar cloths and vestments. Iconoclasts wilfully destroyed such powerful symbols of Catholic orthodoxy, not just in the decades following Henry's break with Rome but also in the period of puritan ascendance in the mid-seventeenth century. As a result, much of English medieval art was destroyed – perhaps as much as 90 per cent according to the art historian Phillip Lindley. Many chantry chapels had patronal images, and examples such as the image of St Gregory at Stoke Charity are especially rare. In many places, the presence of former medieval sculpture is evident in the form of corbels and niches, which formed the architectural setting for images. The survival of such corbels and niches is an important indication that the location of images within and without the church was varied but relied ultimately on being visible from key areas of the church. The eastern gables of the chantry chapels at Bromham and Devizes, for example, were dominated by large niches which once must have held images of the Virgin Mary and would have been clearly visible to those approaching the church (*colour plate 15*). An image niche that related to one of the chapels at St John's in Winchester was placed outside on the east wall of the church, adjacent to a major thoroughfare leading into the city. At St Luke's in Gaddesby, the highly decorated western façade contained a row of narrow blank gables accompanying three large niches, which were highly visible to those entering the church, as were the two large niches on the porch of Bridgwater church, which may have related to the two chantries founded inside it.

Images acted as the focus for either personal or collective devotion. In some cases, the chapel altar may have been spatially associated with the image as a joint devotional focus. In the south chapel at Droxford, the niche was inserted into a particularly narrow space between the chapel altar and the squint that provided a view to the high altar. Here the image was intended to have been visually associated with the respective altars in the chapel and chancel, perhaps a patronal link was set up between the image and the altars. At Urchfont, the niche formed part of a sculptured reredos, which provided an architectural 'frame' for the chapel altar. Images were also painted on chapel screens and these were seen to be no less effective. Some particularly good examples can be found in East Anglia. For example, at the parish church of Barton-Turf, the south chapel has a painted wooden screen depicting the royal saints, St Edward the Confessor, St Olaf of Norway, St Edmund and Henry VI. The unusual royal subject of the screen may suggest that it had a political as well as a religious function, in that it depicted the uncanonised Henry VI (a king the Tudor dynasty was anxious to see canonised) within a lineage of saintly precedents. At Southwold, the south chapel screen depicts Old Testament prophets, whilst that for the north chapel is painted with angels. The screens appear to have been painted by different craftsmen.

Many images in the parish churches comprised wall paintings which also served to illustrate religious stories and events. The survival of images in painted form is particularly rare, though fragmentary evidence does survive from a number of examples. Overall, it seems that religious wall paintings were common, but were to become a major casualty of the Reformation. Where examples do survive they testify to the importance and quality of such adornment. In the parishes churches of Pickering and South Leigh (*colour plate 2*) for instance, one can get a precious insight into what the painted interior of a medieval church may have looked like. Wall paintings cover much of the nave and include religious scenes as well as decorative motifs.

Some wall paintings survive in chantry chapels. Paintings of saints and related events seem to have been particularly prominent. The north and south walls of the Swayne chapel at St Thomas's in Salisbury, for example, depicted scenes from the life of the Virgin, while the chapel of St Katherine in Cirencester has a painting of St Christopher. The east wall of the Hampton chapel at Stoke Charity was painted with various religious scenes. Some wall paintings may have had more personal associations. For example, on the north wall of the chapel of St Anne in Farleigh Hungerford is a remarkable painting of a warlike St George, an image which may particularly reflect the martial connections of the Hungerford founders, who, as well as building the castle there, were also prominent antagonists both in the Hundred Years' War and the War of the Roses. In the Leigh chapel at Godshill, the elaborate painting of Christ on the lily cross depicted on the east wall is particularly striking and as well as being devotional may have also acted as a 'rebus' (*colour plate 20*). It is likely that the 'lily' was a play on words for the name Leigh, such as 'Leigh, Leigh' or 'le Leigh'. If so, then the usage of this depiction becomes more obvious, as it identifies the chapel's founder, John Leigh, whilst juxtaposing his name with the image of Christ – a potentially powerful intercessory tool. Elsewhere, other types of theme included the use of the IHS monogram, representing the name of Christ. At Ewelme and in the Frowyk chantry chapel at South Mimms, evidence survives for the use of IHS motifs on the walls. At Ewelme church, the chapel of St John the Baptist on the south side of the chancel is a beautiful example of rich Perpendicular work (*colour plate 19*). Much of the original decorative scheme survives here, though restored. The roof is panelled and embossed with angels bearing ornamented shields, and the walls are decorated with the IHS monogram in alternate groups of black and red, with texts in Gothic lettering bordering the ceiling. Such an arrangement had a mantra-like effect; the decorative repetition of the name of Christ having a cumulative merit (*45*). Similarly, the inclusion of personal devices or depictions could be juxtaposed with religious symbols and, in the increasingly literate society of the late fifteenth and early sixteenth century, written text. In the Clopton chantry at Long Melford there are faded images of John Clopton and family. Close by, the painted wooden ceiling below has inscribed panels with verses written by John Lydgate (*c.*1450) (*colour plate 21*). One such verse reads 'O Jesus Mercy, with support of Thy grace ... Remember our complaint.

45 Painted monograms, St John's chapel, Ewelme

During our life with many great trespass, by many wrong paths where we have miswent'. Above the tomb of Clopton a painted figure of Christ holding a cross states 'Everyone who lives and believes in me shall never die' again reinforcing the link between pious sentiment and personal intercession.

Often, wall paintings could represent a devotional focus in the chapel. At Ashton, the dominant religious image in the Chudleigh chapel was that of the image of pity, displayed high on the north wall of the chapel, where it could be seen and prayed for by all. The Morduant chantry chapel in the south aisle at

Turvey has a fourteenth-century painting of the crucifixion in a niche on the south wall. It is possible that this was a devotional centrepiece for a local guild, and an altar may have once stood close by. A particularly interesting set of wall paintings survives at Stoke Dry. Here, murals in the Digby chapel, dated to 1280–1284, depict the martydom of St Edmund by Viking bowmen, wearing what looks to be Native American Indian headdresses. This has led some to suggest that this was an early depiction of Indians as brought about by early Viking colonisers. However, many figural depictions in the medieval period feature an assortment of hats and costumes so one should not, perhaps, take such depictions too literally. This is borne out by the painting of St Christopher in the same chapel, which depicts him as an idealised and rather oddly dressed pilgrim.

Many medieval wall paintings, particularly in some of the smaller churches, are in dire need of conservation. Some valuable work has been done and illustrates the importance of such efforts in shedding light on a fast disappearing aspect of ecclesiastical heritage. For example, the wall paintings in the chantry chapel at Farleigh Hungerford have been the subject of a recent project conducted by English Heritage and the Courtauld Institute, London. This work has included photographic and graphic documentation combined with video microscopy, remedial conservation work, moisture distribution surveys and salt analysis. Detailed analysis of the original materials of the wall paintings has also been undertaken and has revealed a highly sophisticated use of translucent glazes over gold and silver leaf and the use of a wide range of pigments including orpiment – natural mineral compounds based on arsenic and sulphur, with oil as a medium.

The survival of stained glass in chantry chapels is particularly rare and is not normally a significant feature of many surviving foundations. However insight can be gained into the nature of this particular art form through the few surviving examples found in parish churches, such as at Fairford and Long Melford. A particularly significant example of medieval stained glass can be found in the domestic chapel at Hengrave Hall where 21 lights of glass created by Flemish craftsmen around 1538 survive intact. The glass, commissioned by Thomas Kytson, depicts the whole history of salvation from the creation of the world to the Last Judgment and is a remarkable survival of its time. Some rare examples of chapel stained glass survive in the Beauchamp chapel, St Mary's in Warwick and at Outwell. Here research by art historian Claire Daunton has traced the influence of Flemish craftsmen in the chantry chapels which feature images of the Black Magi, St Martina and St Faith. An interesting fragmentary example can be found in the west window of the Dauncey chapel at West Lavington. The glass may not be in its original position, but its imagery is nonetheless intact and depicts the ornate gothic 'D' of the founder's family (which also adorns the chapel arches) juxtaposed with a chalice and Eucharistic bread, thus forging a connection between the chapel's founders and the intercessory rituals enacted within.

Parish chantry chapels were unique institutions. Their form, fabric and location were often designed to evoke memory and to attract prayers, as well as to create potent symbols of personal and corporate prestige, piety and influence. However, a central element behind their foundation, whether in monasteries or the parishes, was spatial organisation and the formation of a relationship with other parts of the church. The following chapter will therefore consider the chantry chapel within its ritual topography and discuss how various strategies for the afterlife necessitated the organising, and often reorganising, of a complex network of spatial relationships within the body of the church and within the chapels themselves.

CHAPTER 7

THE SPATIAL ARCHITECTURE OF MEDIEVAL CHANTRY CHAPELS

Behind the foundation of many chantry chapels, considerations of design and architectural embellishment were of prime importance. The same importance was attached to the choice of location: where the chapel fitted in with the ritual 'landscape' of the monastic or parish church, often replete with shrines, altars, monuments and pious devotees. The decoration of chantry chapels, often a synthesis of religious and secular motifs, was designed to draw the attention of the onlooker and to evoke the memory of the deceased, their status and piety, forever. Founders intended such monuments to continue operating for many years after their death, effectively pumping out beneficial masses in perpetuity and making them personalised eternal markers in both time and space. It appears that many chapels were deliberately situated to attract and draw in the prayers of particular groups of individuals. In many instances chantry chapels were located in, and even intruded on, areas of specific religious value and often their internal spaces were organised to reflect specific intercessory strategies. This chapter will examine some of these issues with reference to some of the best surviving examples and illustrate how medieval strategies for the afterlife were not just confined to the structure and design of chantry chapels, but also to their spatial location, internal organisation and wider associations.

CHANTRY CHAPELS: PRIVATISED MONUMENTS IN THE WIDER CONTEXT

Previous work by the author on parish church chantry chapels in the south and west of England has shown that many chapels founded before the fifteenth century were generally located in the more publicly accessible parts of the parish church, such as in the churchyard, nave or aisles. However, from the late fifteenth century onward, there appears to be a trend towards more exclusive locations, such as within or flanking the more prestigious chancel. This may suggest a requirement for more exclusivity. For example, studies conducted on 45 parish church chantry chapels in the county of Somerset show that around 75 per cent of chapels founded after 1400 were located in the area of the chancel. Before 1400, close to 70 per cent of chapel foundations were situated in the nave or transepts. A good example is the Ralegh chapel at Nettlecombe. Founded as a chantry chapel in the late thirteenth century, it took the form of a wide south aisle open to the nave of the church, making it visually and physically part of the church body. However, an additional chapel, added in the 1530s at the east end of the north aisle and connected to the chancel, was of a different nature. It was divided from the aisle by a screen which, together with its location, prioritised its association with the chancel. Likewise the two early sixteenth-century north chapels at Minehead were integral to the chancel and were divided from the western limb of the church by a series of screens. At Montacute, entrance to the chapel from the north porch was via a small lobby to the west of the family chapel, which, like that at Nettlecombe, was positioned next to the chancel. A stairway from the lobby gave exclusive access to a room above the porch. Elsewhere, other examples such as the Spencer chapel at Great Brington and the Greenway chapel at Tiverton, were sectioned off from the main body of the church with iron railings and had their own private entrances.

This trend for exclusivity is seemingly more apparent in monasteries and cathedrals of the period. For example at Winchester Cathedral the chantry chapels of Bishops Wykeham (d.1404) and Edington (d.1366) were located in the nave of the church, as was Bishop Brantyngham's chapel at Exeter cathedral (c.1390). However, at Winchester the chantry chapels of the later fifteenth and early sixteenth-century bishops Beaufort, Fox, Gardiner and Wayneflete were placed in the more exclusive east end of the cathedral (46). Furthermore, the construction of masonry and wooden screens around the choir in the early sixteenth century virtually enclosed these chantry chapels. At Ely Cathedral the chantry chapels of Bishops Alcock (1486-1500) and West (1515-1534) occupied corresponding bays at the extreme east end of the north and south choir aisles and were virtually separate from the choir as well as the nave of the church. More dramatically, at Hereford Cathedral, the two-storey chapel of Bishop Edmund Audley (1492-1502) projected from the south side of the Lady Chapel and gave the impression of being a separate building in its own right. Internally the chapel was almost completely enclosed by panelled screens.

Such trends, it could be claimed, may reveal a move towards the 'privatisation' of religion as posited by some historians, as well as perhaps a shift in the traditional

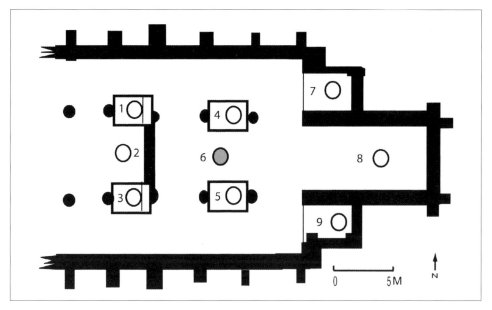

46 Plan of east end of Winchester Cathedral showing location of chantry chapels, altars and shrine: 1) Gardiner chapel, 2) high altar 3) Fox chapel 4) Wayneflete chapel 5) Beaufort chapel 6) site of St Swithun's shrine from the fifteenth century 7) Orleton chapel 8) Lady chapel 9) Langton chapel

emphasis placed on public participation in such monuments. According to Thomson, the years after 1450 saw the highest numbers of land enclosures and therefore wider social trends towards appropriation and privacy may be reflected in the increased privatisation of parish and monastic church space. This may indicate a perceived trend towards exclusivity as reflected in the foundation of particular chantry chapels. However, the idea that chapels were situated in the east end of churches for reasons of exclusivity and privacy is simplistic and there were many exceptions. The chantry chapel of Walter, Lord Hungerford (1429) now in the choir of Salisbury Cathedral, was originally in the north arcade of the nave. The Neville chantry at Durham Cathedral was constructed in the nave's south aisle in the second decade of the fifteenth century. The fact that these two examples were founded by laymen may suggest the reasons behind their location in the traditional 'lay' area of the cathedrals. However this it seems was not the universal rule. For example, at the former Augustinian priory at Bristol (now the cathedral) the Berkeley chapel founded in 1348 projects southward from the choir and is almost like a separate, exclusive adjunct to the choir, whilst at Exeter Cathedral the Courtenay chantry chapel (now in the south transept) of 1375 was originally in the nave. However, it should be noted that the Berkeley family had been particularly generous patrons of the priory since its foundation and this

47 Chantry chapel
of Humphrey of
Gloucester and site
of St Alban's shrine
(in the foreground),
St Albans Abbey

may have warranted a special position for the family's chapel. Likewise, Duke
Humphrey of Gloucester, who had a special affiliation with the cathedral and
shrine at St Alban's abbey, had his chantry constructed close to the saint's shrine,
a position of prime importance (47). As noted at Winchester, some ecclesiastics
also chose to locate their chantry chapels within the naves of their churches. At
Norwich Cathedral, the chantry chapel of Bishop Richard Nyke (1501-1536) was
in the south aisle of the nave; at Wells Cathedral, the fifteenth-century Bubwith
and Sugar chapels were to the north and south side of the nave respectively.

Likewise in the parish churches, many chapels and chantries of the fifteenth
and sixteenth centuries were still founded in more public areas of the church,
such as the early sixteenth-century Horton and Birde chantries in the nave aisle
at Bradford-on-Avon and the Lane aisle at Cullompton. Undoubtedly, evidence

for later chantry chapels founded within church naves, such as at Burford and Chipping Norton, suggests the former presence of many more.

It therefore appears that any apparent trend to found chantries in the more easterly areas of churches cannot just be put down to a desire for restriction and privacy. Certainly an association with such areas contained a degree of elitism and privilege. However, the desire for some testators to found their chantries in the comparatively more exclusive choirs and chancels was more to do with the association with areas of potential spiritual efficacy than mere 'privacy'. Those chapels founded within the naves and other publicly accessible areas were highly visual and therefore prestigious, and were able to draw on the wider prayers of the public. However, chapels founded in the choirs and chancels were able to draw from the efficacy of the high altar – the prime spiritual focus – and the devout prayers of the choir monks, as well as from association with holy relics, saints' shrines and the traffic of pilgrims. Those at Ely, Hereford and Salisbury Cathedrals were positioned close to Lady Chapels. As we have seen, the Virgin Mary played a particularly prominent role in intercessory practice. Overall, there appears not to have been a universally 'favoured' location within the church; we see a certain amount of freedom in chantry location, based perhaps on individual motives and responses to the afterlife, as well as, it should be noted, on the spatial and architectural constraints of the church. Such strategies for the afterlife were perhaps dependent on personal beliefs and opinion regarding what would be the most efficacious location. Here we see individual agency at work – like the design and decoration of their chantry chapels, many founders appear to have had differing personal motives and different views on the location of their monuments, as well as what would make an effective strategy for the afterlife.

With regard to more unusual locations for chapel foundation, sometimes these personal motives may be lost to us. For example, the sixteenth-century Sylke chantry at Exeter Cathedral is located in what would appear to be an obscure corner of the north transept. Sylke was cathedral precentor and it may be that this space was deemed appropriate for a man of his status. However, it may also be that the precentor had a particular affiliation with this place; there may have been a favoured altar or nearby image, which may have influenced his choice of location. The chantry chapels of Edington and Wykeham at Winchester were located in the rebuilt nave, and that of Bishop Langley (*c.*1414) in the western 'Galilee' chapel at Durham Cathedral – all works they were associated with and wished to be remembered for.

In cathedrals, one of the most popular locations was close to a saint's shrine, a location which not only made a statement of privilege but, more importantly, meant proximity to the empowered remains of a saint whose personal intercessory powers could be relied upon.

SAINTS' SHRINES AND CHANTRY CHAPEL LOCATION

The veneration of saints is closely linked to the medieval theme of pilgrimage. Pilgrimage was an important component of late medieval religion and pilgrimage to holy sites was another strategy through which remission of sins could be obtained. Again, such remission was actually accountable and reckoned in days. For example, a pilgrimage to Santiago de Compostela in Spain could earn a remission of a third of one's sins. If one happened to die on the way (for many it was a long journey) total remission was given. In 1350, Pope Clement VI encouraged the faithful to make a pilgrimage to Rome to obtain a plenary jubilee indulgence. Again if one died on the way, total remission was guaranteed (here, one cannot fail to see the exploitative link between promises in the afterlife and self-serving martyrdom – a belief which has dramatic and fatal echoes even today). Significantly, the following year a cash payment could be provided instead of making the journey. It was also possible for people to pay for a pilgrimage to be done and as consequence 'professional pilgrims' began to appear and to travel around collecting indulgences for their patrons. The sale of indulgences was to become one of the more obvious and odious mechanisms through which the medieval church could raise funds and the more cynical among us cannot fail to see why the church's ratification of purgatory was so lucrative.

The most important pilgrim centres were Jerusalem, Rome and Santiago de Compostela, but England also had her own internationally important shrines, such as those of St Thomas Becket at Canterbury and St Swithun at Winchester, among other examples. A visit to such shrines was seen as spiritually meritorious, while to be buried close to a shrine was thought to be of equally great spiritual benefit for the soul. The close spatial relationship between chantry and shrine would create a direct spiritual benefit from the physical remains of the saint, who could intercede personally on behalf of the deceased. Just as importantly, however, this was a location that made a statement of piety: here, one was in the company of saints. The shrines themselves in turn attracted numerous pilgrims who could also be petitioned to pray for the individual represented by the chantry foundation.

At Winchester Cathedral, the two free-standing chantry chapels of Bishops Wayneflete (*c.*1480s) and Beaufort (*c.*1440s) effectively stood guard over the shrine of St Swithun (*colour plate 22*). Unfortunately, the shrine monument is now lost, but it is not hard to conjecture that the surviving tall and imposing chapels of the two bishops must have reduced its architectural significance somewhat. A similar example can be seen at Westminster Abbey, where the H-shaped two-storied chapel of Henry V (*c.*1422) dominated the space around the shrine of

Edward the Confessor (*48*). Furthermore, the construction of the chapel must have caused significant changes to the layout of the saint's shrine. Reliquaries and the Trinity altar had to be removed and some damage was caused to the surrounding tombs. The giant 'H' of the chapel's design also imposed itself visually on any onlookers viewing the shrine. Some 70 years later, Henry VII was causing similar disturbances with the erection of his magnificent chapel, which replaced the earlier Lady Chapel at Westminster. This chapel was originally intended to house the relics of Henry VI whom Henry VII had tried, but ultimately failed, to get canonised.

At Lincoln Cathedral the chantry chapels of Bishops Fleming (*49*) (*c*.1425), Russell (*c*.1494) and Longland (*c*.1540s) were placed around the shrine of St Hugh, but did not dominate the space in the same way as those at Winchester or Westminster. Indeed they seem to keep a respectful distance, flanking the north and south walls of the church's east end (*50*). However, the chapels of Longland and Russell are situated on either side of the south porch that gave access to the sacred area. In this location, framing the portal, they were still highly visible, although distinctly less intrusive, and interestingly, anyone entering via the porch could not have helped but see the chantry chapel of Bishop Fleming directly behind the shrine of St Hugh. At St Albans, the two-storey chapel of Duke Humphrey of Gloucester is located to the south of St Alban's shrine, whilst his body was buried under the pavement of the saint's chapel. At Salisbury Cathedral, the chantry chapels of Bishop Richard Beauchamp and Robert Hungerford were founded and constructed within a decade or so of the canonisation of St Osmund and flanked the area to which his shrine was translated some time after 1457.

The relationship between chantry chapels and shrines can be further illustrated at Canterbury Cathedral, with the relationship between the tomb and chantry chapel of Henry IV and the shrine of Thomas Becket. Some historians have suggested that during the later years of his reign, King Henry was filled with remorse and guilt both for his usurpation and, possibly, his implication in the murder of Richard II and, later, the execution of Archbishop Scrope of York in 1405. Henry's diminutive and unpretentious chantry chapel at Canterbury is arguably more indicative of a noble than of a royal personage, and certainly not the founder of a royal dynasty. The size of the chapel, and its modest decoration, point to a certain level of reservation, or even humility, behind its design. This is especially noticeable when it is compared to other contemporary royal foundations. The fact that Henry wished to be buried at Canterbury and not at the traditional royal resting place of Westminster might suggest that here was a man who perhaps deemed himself unfit to reside in such a place, choosing instead to reside next to the powerful intercessory influence of Becket's shrine, rather than that of the saintly and royal King Edward the Confessor. Henry's

Above: 48 Chantry chapel of Henry V and site of Edward the Confessor's shrine (Courtesy of Dean and Chapter of Westminster Abbey)

Opposite above: 49 Fleming chapel, Lincoln Cathedral

Opposite below: 50 Plan of east end of Lincoln Cathedral: 1) high altar 2) site of shrine of St Hugh 3) Fleming chapel 4) Longland chapel 5) Russell chapel 6) south door

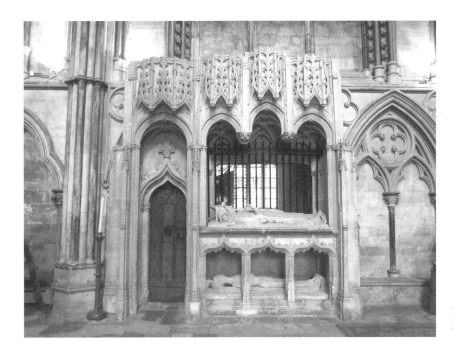

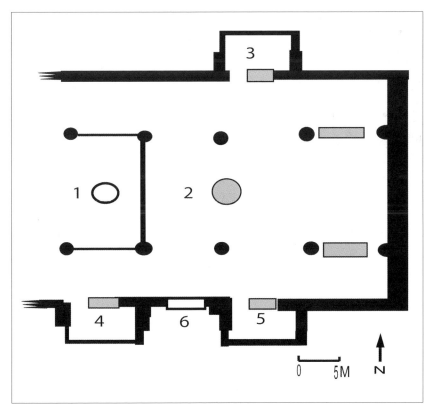

chronic ill health and general state of mind in the years leading up to his death may have meant that his chapel and tomb represented a penitential piety extending into the afterlife.

Geoffrey Cook has suggested that location by a saint's shrine was the most favoured position for chantry foundation. As we have seen previously, the intercession of saints on behalf of the soul was of particular benefit. However, it appears that not every founder favoured this particular location and other areas, such as the high altar or places of high visibility, were to them equally or even more important.

CHANTRY CHAPELS AND THE HIGH ALTAR

The construction of chantry chapels close to the high altar brought them near to the central religious focus of the church and, in monasteries, often close to the monks' choir; a place where regular prayer and observations would be performed throughout the day and night. For example, at St Albans' Abbey, despite available space in the saint's chapel, Abbots William Wallingford (*c*.1480) and John Wheathampstead (*c*.1464) chose to construct their chapels in the presbytery just to the north and south of the high altar. Examples of impressive chapels built close to high altars include that of Prior William Birde (*c*.1515) at the former Benedictine abbey of Bath, and Bishop Audley (*c*.1520), flanking the high altar at Salisbury Cathedral. A particularly noteworthy example is the Salisbury chapel at Christchurch Priory. The chantry chapel built for the Countess of Salisbury, Margaret de la Pole, was founded around 1520 and was positioned so that it protruded into the sanctuary. Occupying the raised dais, it was literally only a metre or so away from the high altar and occupied a place of great prestige and high visibility (*colour plate 23*). As such it operated as a backdrop to the high altar and 'triggered' the awareness of the monks entering the choir from the south aisle and cloister. At Tewkesbury Abbey, a cluster of closely grouped cage chantries provided a physical cordon around the site of the high altar (*51 & 52*). Access was still possible, of course, but one is left in no doubt about the status and precedence of these monuments and, importantly, the individuals they represented.

Often such foundations could physically obstruct light, vision or physical access to such important areas. One dramatic example of the effect of such appropriation of space can be seen at Worcester Cathedral. Here the tomb of Bishop Godfrey Giffard (*c*.1302) was set by the bishop's direction on the south side of the high altar sanctuary. Giffard's tomb was apparently a particularly high structure which interfered with the ceremonial at the altar and also shut out

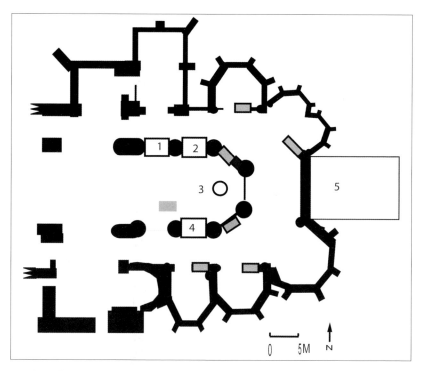

51 Plan of east end of Tewkesbury Abbey: 1) Warwick chapel 2) Fitzhamon chapel 3) high altar 4) Trinity 'Despenser' chapel 5) site of Lady chapel

52 Chantry chapels and high altar (to the right of the picture), Tewkesbury Abbey

much light. Even though this was his tomb, the bishop was indirectly enforcing a type of chantry by making his memorial both visually and physically connected with the most important ritual focus in the church. However, happily, later appeals by the community led to its removal.

Medieval Christian ideology, as applied to ecclesiastical buildings, ordained that the east end of the church was especially spiritually efficacious, thanks to its orientation towards the Holy Land. Many churches faced eastward and their altars were positioned at the east end. This particular emphasis on an easterly orientation may explain why the construction of some chapels involved the extension of various parts of the eastern end of churches and cathedrals. At times this may have set up a spatial rivalry between chapels and choirs or chancels. For example, at Ely, the construction of the West chantry chapel (c.1533) in the east end of the south choir aisle entailed the building of a new east wall some metres further eastward, making the chapel the easternmost appendage of the church. In contrast, at the parish church of Corsham, it was the church chancel that was extended by half a bay in the fifteenth century so that it projected more easterly than the attached chapel to the north (53). The architectural similarity between the chancel extension and the chapel suggests that this arrangement was contemporary. At St Thomas' in Salisbury, the south aisle was probably extended

53 Tropenell chapel, Corsham church

by three bays in the fifteenth century to facilitate the founding of two chantries. Naturally, the reasons behind this could be simply to provide more space, but it is equally likely that a desire to place these chantries nearer to the high altar and its rituals was also a prime requisite.

At St John's in Winchester, the alignment of squints providing views to the chancel high altar for the priests serving the subsidiary altars in the north and south chapels is of particular interest. As discussed in more detail below, the presence and alignment of squints can tell us much about the former position of priests (and therefore their altars) and enables the reconstruction of the liturgical layout. At St John's, the squint alignments suggest that the north and particularly the south altar were aligned slightly to the west of the high altar (*54*). This arrangement can also be seen in many other examples, notably at Buckland Dinham and Old Basing. Such particular arrangements may simply indicate the former presence of obstructions such as altar rails or steps. Alternatively, they may imply that there was a requirement to position chantry and chapel altars slightly to the west of the high altar, thus respecting the spiritual integrity of the church and indicating that some parish church chantries were not intended to 'rock the boat' by infringing, or attempting to replace, the priority of the parish's main ritual focus.

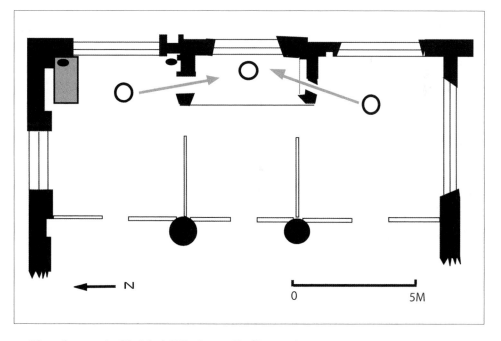

54 Plan of east end of St John's, Winchester (Roffey 2007)

CHANTRY CHAPELS AND PROCESSIONAL ROUTES

On certain occasions, such as Easter Week and Feast Days, the medieval church was the setting for processions often involving both the lay and religious communities. In the monasteries, every Sunday a holy-water procession involved the sprinkling of the high altar and the other altars of the church, as well as other ritual areas. Often, consecration crosses marked the route and stations of the church processions, as at Salisbury Cathedral. In some parish churches, secondary or so-called processional aisles were added, such as at St Mary Magdalene in Taunton and at Cullompton, which also housed chantry foundations. The frequency and variety of religious processions in medieval Christian worship allowed different social groups to move into and around the discrete spaces of the church. The location of chantry chapels in these areas was therefore of some consequence. In some cases, such as at the chantry chapels in the parish churches at Avebury, Portbury and Sherston, so-called processional squints (effectively small internal doorways, discussed below) facilitated movement between chapels and other spaces of the church, making these chapels into 'gateways' for the processional traffic. Furthermore, in those monasteries and cathedrals that were important pilgrim centres, ambulatories allowed the pilgrims to process around the church en route to paying their respects to the shrine normally housed in the eastern arm of the church. Hence the series of chantry chapels at Winchester Cathedral and Christchurch Priory, among others; these effectively lined the processional ambulatories of their churches and capitalised on the procession of pilgrims and clergy moving through these spaces.

One important consideration was that chantry chapels located within the nave of monastic churches could also be positioned close to the cloister entrance. As such they would be readily visible to the monks entering and leaving the cloister to fulfil religious observances. At Southwark Priory (now Southwark Cathedral) the Gower chantry was located in the north aisle at the east end of the nave of the priory church. Here it was regularly visible from all parts of the nave. However, it was also next to the so-called 'prior's doorway', a main entrance from the cloister into the body of the church (55). Therefore the chapel and tomb would be highly visible. Here the power of the tomb as memorial and the chantry as a vehicle for intercession was greatly enhanced by the attention of the religious. Similar arrangements existed with regard to the Courtenay chapel at Exeter Cathedral, the Bridport chapel at Salisbury Cathedral and that of Bishop Edington at Winchester. Excavations at the Austin Friary in Winchester revealed a series of burials placed at the cloister entrance, again testifying to the importance of memorial location. A central aspect behind many of these foundations is clearly the importance of vision and the facility for visual accessibility. We shall now examine this in more detail.

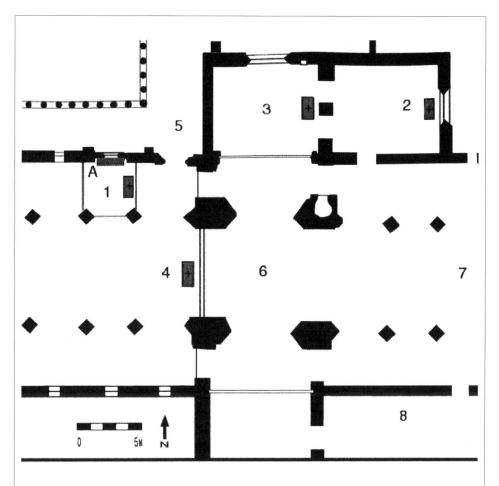

1 The Chapel of St John the Baptist & Gower chantry with
  tomb (A)
2 Chapel of St John the Evangelist
3 Chapel of St Peter
4 Nave altar & rood screen
5 Cloister
6 Choir
7 Sanctuary
8 Chapel of St Mary Magdalene

55 Plan of Gower chantry chapel and other altars, Southwark Cathedral (drawn by author, from Hines, Cohen and Roffey 2004)

CHANTRY CHAPELS AND PUBLIC VISIBILITY

Many chantry chapels were founded in important ritual and prestigious areas, undoubtedly so as to attach an element of status and privilege to the chapels and, by association, their founder. In a sense, such foundations were distancing themselves from the various networks of rituals and observations being carried out in the main bodies of their churches. Unlike other examples discussed below, it is reasonably clear that the sanctuary chapels of Wayneflete and Beaufort at Winchester Cathedral, and similar examples, contributed little to religious practices carried out in the main areas of the church, i.e. the choir and nave. Chantry chapels located in the naves of churches made highly visible statements, but importantly, they and their masses were also accessible to the wider public. Therefore, although they may have contributed relatively little to the main religious practice at the high altar, they made a significant contribution to the religious experience of the laity. A unique example can be seen in the north chapel at Asthall (56). Unusually, the altar is located at the southern edge of the chapel. The altar itself is remarkable, with the altar table, masonry frame and attached piscina all surviving. Its particular location to the south of the chapel, however, meant that it was easily viewed from the north aisle. In addition, the serving priest could also see the high altar through the chapel south arch. This arrangement suggests that visual accessibility was a prime factor in the spatial arrangements of this chapel. Furthermore, the survival of medieval altars in chapels is rare and the example at Asthall may testify to this arrangement having been more common than previously thought. For example, the squint from the Wadham chapel in the north transept at Ilminster church is located at the south end of the chapel. The squint contains a piscina and it is therefore likely that the altar was close to this point. If so, then it was situated so as to be clearly seen from the north aisle – in a more central location it would be obscured (57). Such arrangements made divine worship more accessible to the general laity and brought the mass more into the public domain.

Commonly the chantry mass was a 'morrow mass', held at dawn for those who generally worked during the day when the high mass was normally celebrated, and as such it may have provided for the majority of the laity. An important aspect of the religious practices performed within the chapels and chantries, and a factor that was crucial in the interactions between the laity and the intercessory rituals, was the association of the masses celebrated in the chapels with specified individuals, especially the chapel or chantry founders. Very broadly speaking, the attraction of the chapels and chantries on a purely spiritual level was that they were a context for the mass. 'Presencing mechanisms' allowed the mass to be associated with the individual by the use of various associative devices such as

56 Asthall church showing the view to the chapel altar from the north aisle

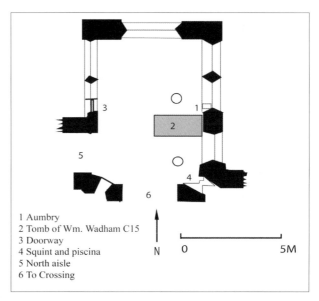

1 Aumbry
2 Tomb of Wm. Wadham C15
3 Doorway
4 Squint and piscina
5 North aisle
6 To Crossing

N   0   5M

57 Wadham chapel, Ilminster church, showing location of former altars (Roffey 2007)

tombs, heraldic devices and symbols, and in the form of inscribed altar cloths and wall hangings. The fact that many chapels and chantries were used by founders and later family members during their lives does not detract from the function of such institutions as primarily intercessory foundations. The 'active' role and presence of the founders, it can be argued, could have continued post-mortem, in that the deceased ensured a presence in their chapels by symbolism, memorials and especially the ritual itself. The announcement of the name of the deceased was more than simple recollection – it was the means by which the dead were made present.

CHANTRIES, CHAPELS AND VISUAL TOPOGRAPHY

As we have seen, the spiritual prominence of the mass in popular religion of the period was paramount. It was the most important element of religious practice in the monasteries and those monks who were also priests were required to celebrate it every day. We have also discussed that, for the laity, the main medium for the communication of religious experience was through the visual sense, particularly with regard to the mass and the direct visual communion with the host at the point of elevation. Therefore, what can be seen in many, if not the majority, of instances is that an essential requirement of chantry and chapel planning was to provide for clear sight-lines into the chapels from general areas of the church. Importance was placed upon direct visual communion with the elevation, but also upon indirect visual contact with the symbolic elements of the chapel, through its rituals, its decoration and its architectural embellishment.

We may see a contradiction here. Despite some being located in visually accessible areas, the majority of chapels were screened. Most screens hid much of the inside of the chapel from view, including often both the altar and the celebrant priest. However, the top levels of many screens were open, pierced by windows or grilles, and did not therefore hide the most essential element of the ritual: the elevation. At Durham Cathedral, a contemporary account informs us that the Neville chantry in the south aisle was enclosed at each end by 'a little stone wall', that on the east side being 'somewhat higher than the altar'. This arrangement and others similar would preserve the propriety and mystery of the mass, and the various gesticulations of the priest, whilst allowing the elevation to be seen. At Lincoln Cathedral, the three chantry chapels that occupied the great south transept had partial screens which delineated each foundation, but did not hinder visibility between them (*58*).

Evidence for the insertion of 'peep-holes' or small elevation squints in some church screens, such those in the screen of the north chapel, South Leigh (*59*) and

58 Chapels in the south greater transept, Lincoln Cathedral. Here the fore-shortened screens defined individual space but allowed for visual accessibility between respective altars. Furthermore, the now blocked doorway through to the aisle would have once provided a view to an altar in the nave screen (see *67*)

in the wooden Spring chapel at Lavenham, allowed those kneeling close to the screen, or children, to observe the elevation. The unorthodox insertion of these small holes reveals the ability of the general laity to negotiate such barriers, as well as an apparent tolerance and certain flexibility on the part of the clergy. The peep-holes in the screens in the Huse chapel in Cheddar and to the north chapel at St John's in Winchester indicate that the insertion of such breaches was reasonably unrestrained. At South Leigh, the peep-holes are intricately carved architectural features. In these examples, the comparative intricacy, and therefore the time taken to insert these, could not have gone unnoticed. This is not to say that they were countenanced, but they were probably tolerated. There is even evidence that this factor was incorporated into later screen design, as at Roxton and Cherry Hinton. At Winchester Cathedral, the chantry chapel of Bishop Thomas Langton (*c.*1500) in the south-east corner of the retrochoir has a remarkable wooden canopied screen with a built-in sedilia (seating for the officiating clergy) (*16*). The screen

59 South Leigh church showing elevation squints or 'peep holes' inserted into the chapel screen. Note prayer desk by right-hand squint

itself incorporated small peep-holes to facilitate vision into the chapel from the retrochoir. The example at Lavenham raises another question. The interior of the chapel would have been visible from most of the large, spacious nave. Are we to assume, therefore, that on certain occasions the church was so crammed full of people that those kneeling close to the chapels did not otherwise have a view of the elevation? This is unlikely. The holes could be for the benefit of children or, more likely, for parishioners who wanted to get as close as possible to the chapel and also required an unrestricted view whilst kneeling. If so, this suggests an almost shrine-like quality to these monuments. At South Leigh, the screen squint was located close to a prayer-desk and may have been used for private devotional practice. At St Cuthbert's in Wells, the wall between the chapel of the Holy Trinity and the chapel of St Katherine to its east contains a window. This window was formerly external (before the latter chapel was added), but was likely kept to provide visual access into the new chapel. A similar arrangement may also be found in the south chapel of St Thomas at Burford.

60 The twelfth-century squint at Compton church, among one of the earliest in the country

VISUAL RELATIONSHIPS AND CHAPEL TOPOGRAPHY

Achieving clear sight-lines in a church interior often obstructed by walls and monuments was potentially problematic. To alleviate this problem, and to secure good lines of visual communication both between altars and between altars and public areas, squints were often used (*60*). For the study of religious practice within the medieval church, the position of squints and their relation to other areas of the church can reveal much about the spatial relationship between chantry chapels and the rest of church space. Essentially the squint was a small internal window that facilitated a view where otherwise it would be obstructed, such as through walls or arcade piers, and it is particularly common to the parish church, though there are several cathedral examples.

Despite some being architectural features in their own right, such as the decorated three-light squint window at Chipping Norton church, generally squints are quite plain and often appear as a small rectangular insertion, such as the poorly cut examples in the Berkeley chapel at Christchurch Priory (*61*), the small slits in the Grosseteste chapel in Lincoln Cathedral, and in the Markham chapel in the parish church at Newark (*62*). When not used, many may have been hidden behind a small curtain. As discussed by this author elsewhere, the variety of squint types, their size and location, when viewed collectively, suggest that they were used for a variety of functions dependent on their architectural or topographical context. Contrary to common tradition, they cannot have been features that allowed lepers to observe the mass detached from the main community in the nave; the presence of squints in chantry chapels does not support this interpretation. Some squints were small, such as those found between the chancel and chancel chapels at Old Basing, and in the east wall of the cage chantry at Newark. Others were relatively large, such as the substantial aisle squints found at Hambledon, Woodton and West Chiltington, for example, which were clearly used to provide visual access to the high altar for laity in the aisle.

At Long Melford, a squint provided a visual link between the priests serving the Clopton chapel and the Clopton chantry. Here, Eamon Duffy notes that the altar at the east end of the north aisle was provided with a double squint to enable the priest to 'see across the rear angle of the Clopton chantry and through the north wall of the chancel to the exact centre of the high altar'. At Aldbourne, a double squint in the north chapel allowed guild members in the chapel and laity in the aisle to view the high altar. The insertion of a passage squint at Sherston involved the construction of a purpose-built extension to facilitate both visual and physical access between the north chapel and chancel (*63*). The construction of the north aisle and associated chantry foundations at Bridgwater also included the provision of a squint in the east wall of the porch, providing a view to both the chantries and the high altar. The six-metre long squint between the Horton chapel and the chancel at Holy Trinity in Bradford-on-Avon, cut through solid masonry, is a significant feat of engineering (*72*). This particular example indicates the lengths that people would go to make sure vision between altars was achieved.

The majority of squints were oriented roughly east-west to provide a view to high altars. However, some were oriented north-south, as at Bradford-on-Avon, Churchill and Urchfont. These provided a view across the church, focusing on the altars in the nave or other chapels thus suggesting a visual relationship between subsidiary altars. Not all squints were used within chapels or aisles; for example at St Oswald's in Sowerby, a squint was provided in the east wall of the tower to provide a view into the body of the church. At Brympton d'Evercy, Great Chalfield and Yatton, the chapel squints are quite low, only around a metre above the floor level. Furthermore the view they provided to the high altar in the chancel could only be gained from the western end of the chapels. This suggests

61 Squint in the east wall of the Berkeley chapel, Christchurch Priory

62 Squints in east wall of Markham chapel, Newark church

63 Passage squint, Sherston church (Roffey 2006)

that the squints were used by a distinct set of individuals, who were kneeling or perhaps seated at the back of the chapel. It is possible that this represented an area reserved for a distinct group of people who had visual access to both the high altar and the chapel altar. At Brympton d'Evercy, this position was the only spot in the church that provided a view of all the altars in the church and was therefore a position of some prestige.

The visual relationship between chantry chapels is more noticeable in the parish churches than in their monastic counterparts, as is the presence of squints. This may signal a particular emphasis on proximity to other religious foci, such as shrines and high altars, in monasteries, at the expense of general visual access, or, as many of the surviving examples are those of the nobility, perhaps a desire for prestigious location and exclusivity was the priority. Furthermore, many of the cathedrals and monasteries had multiple altars, chantry or otherwise. These were swept away at the Reformation, making the reconstruction of such prior relationships difficult. Generally speaking, the broader, more open spaces of many monastic churches may have facilitated lines of sight more easily than the often cramped parish church interior. However, some evidence does survive for visual relationship between monastic chantry altars at Christchurch Priory. Built in 1486 for Sir William Berkeley, the Berkeley chantry chapel is situated in the

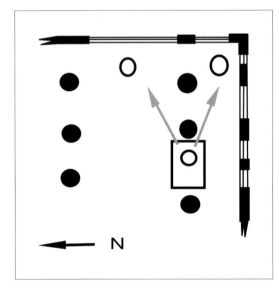

Above: 64 Squints in east wall of de la Warr chapel, Boxgrove Priory

Left: 65 Plan of de la Warr chapel, Boxgrove Priory, showing visual relationships between chapel, Lady Chapel and high altar

north choir aisle. Inside the chapel are two small square squints which would have originally provided a view to the high altar for the officiating priest. However, there is another small square squint on the north-east corner of the chapel, which provided a similar view past the Salisbury chantry and onto a now removed altar in the north choir aisle. At Boxgrove Priory, the de la Warr cage chantry (*colour plate 24*) in the sanctuary south arcade has two squints within its east wall (*64*). One gave a view to the high altar for the chantry priest and the other a view to the Lady Chapel altar at the east end of the south aisle (*65*). At Westminster Abbey, the Islip chantry chapel had a squint that provided a view to the chapel of St John the Baptist to the east. This latter chapel also had a rather enigmatic squint inserted in the entry passage suggesting a visual relationship between here and the chapel interior. Bishop John Stanbury's chantry (*c.*1474) in the choir north aisle at Hereford Cathedral has a low-level squint that facilitated a view to the high altar. The squint is only a few centimetres off the chapel floor and it is hard to imagine the chantry priest adopting a rather undignified posture in attempting to peer through it. It is therefore likely that it was for an assistant or altar boy. A similar low-level squint, also only a few centimetres from the floor, exists in the arcade between the north choir aisle and choir at Norwich Cathedral (the viewer would have been literally laying on the ground). This may mark the former presence of an altar on the site or alternatively a spot from which to view, or keep watch, over the Easter sepulchre, located in the adjacent choir, during Easter week.

In some instances there is some evidence to suggest that certain chantries were linked into a wider visual network of altars and that there was a series of visual relationships between chapel altars. For example, at Lincoln Cathedral the three aforementioned chantry chapels in the south great transept were visually interlinked. There is also evidence to suggest that there was a line of sight from these chapels to a chapel in the pulpitum (nave screen) to the north. This chapel has not been identified, but the presence of a blocked doorway in the south wall of the transept and a small window (in a decorated recess) in the north wall of the pulpitum (*66*) suggests not only the presence of a pulpitum chapel, but also a visual connection between them (*67*). The conjectured location of a chantry chapel in a church pulpitum is not unfounded, as the chantry of Bishop Gower at St David's Cathedral is in such a location (*23*).

St David's itself offers a particularly useful example that further demonstrates the visual relationship between altars. Here, rather unusually, a small squint provided a view from the high altar to the altar in the Vaughan chantry to the east. Furthermore, squint windows in the Vaughan chapel provided a view to the Lady Chapel and possibly also to the chapels of St Nicholas and St Edward at the east end of the choir aisles. It is also likely that the high altar was visible from the Gower chantry chapel in the pulpitum at the east end of the nave. It is therefore clear that at St David's a clear visual relationship existed between the altars, linking them into a complex spiritual network (*68*). However, the squint between the chapel and high altar raises a series of questions. Commonly in such examples the high altar had visual prominence, but here the squint between the high altar and the Vaughan chapel appears to suggest that it was a requirement for the priest at the high altar to see into the Vaughan chapel. Yet, the squint itself is only decorated on one side, that of the Vaughan chapel, which suggests that it was actually a feature of the chapel and was used by the chapel priest. Moreover, the squint on the chapel west wall was clearly too small to be seen through from the chapel altar situated opposite on the east wall (*69 & 70*). To be used effectively, somebody, perhaps an altar boy, would have had to be close to it. Significantly, it

66 Squint through to nave screen chapel from south aisle and transept, Lincoln Cathedral

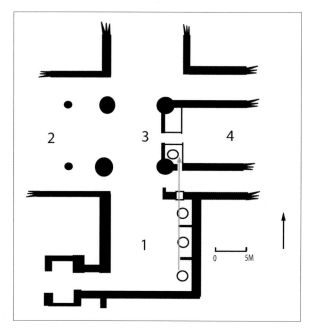

67 Plan of south transept and nave at Lincoln Cathedral showing conjectured visual relationships between chapel altars

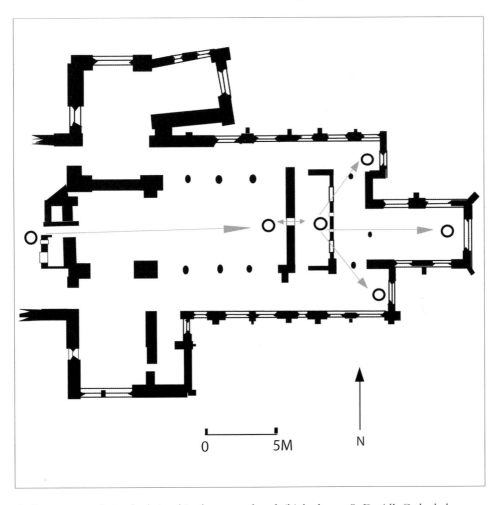

68 Reconstructed visual relationships between chapels/high altar at St David's Cathedral

is also from this position that the chapels of St Nicholas and St Edward could be seen. When we consider some other monastic examples, such as the arrangement of known chantry chapels at Salisbury, Tewkesbury and Winchester Cathedrals, there was clearly a visual relationship between many foundations, suggesting, it can be argued, that a prime consideration behind many chantry chapels was that their masses were linked into a wider ritual network.

It is clear that the chapels in these examples were a component in what can be termed a 'spiritual network' of chapels, each chapel a landmark in a wider ritual landscape. Therefore we cannot always see chantry chapels as stand-alone, exclusive monuments. In many cases they clearly operated within a wider religious context and were components of an inclusive ritual layout.

69 St David's Cathedral. High altar squint (with candle inside) looking east

70 St David's Cathedral. High altar squint looking west from Vaughan chapel

A 'SPIRITUAL NETWORK': CHAPELS, CHANTRIES AND THE PARISH CHURCH

The visual relationship between chantry chapels and between chapels and the high altar is somewhat clearer with regard to chantries founded within parish churches. Here, squints were often used as a visual aid to the staggering of elevations between altars. As a result of the multiplication of masses within a church, including those celebrated within chapels and chantries, the high altar may have been beginning to lose precedence. The chantry mass was a 'low' mass and therefore shorter and, as we have seen, often celebrated early in the morning. A proliferation of altars in the parish church may therefore have led to the staggering of masses so that the laity was not able to evade attending the longer parish mass. Consequently, masses celebrated at side-altars were timed so that their elevations were synchronised. This may imply an order of precedence, further indicating that each priest needed to view the preceding elevation. It is unlikely, however, that such events occurred on a regular basis, particularly in the smaller, rural churches that may have had only one priest, perhaps two, celebrating once a day. Nonetheless, the presence of particular squints in some examples, as noted, suggests a visual relationship between altars. Such relationships should not just be viewed as strictly hierarchical in the sense of clerical control of lay-founded or subsidiary altars. It may alternatively be argued that these relationships were wholly beneficial to the community: the sacred areas of the church, be it chapel, chantry or high altar, were linked into a common and universal structure, which further bonded the community in its religious practices. In this sense the various altars were 'networked' into the web of communal piety. Orders of precedence, ultimately linked to high altars, encouraged a unified approach to the common goal of Eucharistic celebration and the promise of salvation inherent within. Such an order must have been carefully worked out to ensure that timing and visual access were integrated and the dramatic continuity of the various performances ran seamlessly and with chronological precision. Orders of precedence between altars can be deduced from contemporary documents from the larger monastic institutions. For example, Kathleen Edwards noted that the chapters at St Paul's in London and at York Minster arranged times when different masses should be celebrated and consequently, 'if one cantarist did not begin his mass immediately the preceding cantarist had finished, he would be cited before the chapter to answer for neglect'. At secular cathedrals, timetables were drawn up for priests celebrating masses at various altars. At Salisbury Cathedral, the chapter drew up an annual table of *missae currentes*, arranging that those chaplains who were not also vicars choral should celebrate their daily masses successively at the different cathedral altars. Clearly the arrangement of squints between the aforementioned chapels at Christchurch Priory, Lincoln Cathedral and possibly Boxgrove Priory suggests an order of precedence between subsidiary altars.

A prime example of such a complex spiritual network can be seen at Cirencester parish church, where a visual relationship between altars was facilitated by the use of squints in the chapels of St Catherine, Our Lady and the Trinity, as well as the now blocked squint in the chapel of St John the Baptist (*71*). The eastern frame of the wooden parclosed Garstang chapel stops just short of the wall, providing a 'squint' with a view to the high altar via the altar in the chapel of St John the Baptist. However, these visual relationships were not just confined to that between subsidiary altars and the high altars. Orders of precedence also existed between subsidiary altars themselves. At Chipping Norton, the elaborate three-light painted squint at the altar of St Nicholas in the western part of St Catherine's chapel was constructed to provide a direct view to the Lady Chapel. The squint in the east wall of the Markham chapel at Newark provided a view to the chapel in the east end of the chancel south aisle (*62*). A particularly interesting arrangement can be seen at Churchill. In the north chapel, the south-facing squint provided a view to the opposite south chapel altars, whilst the east squint

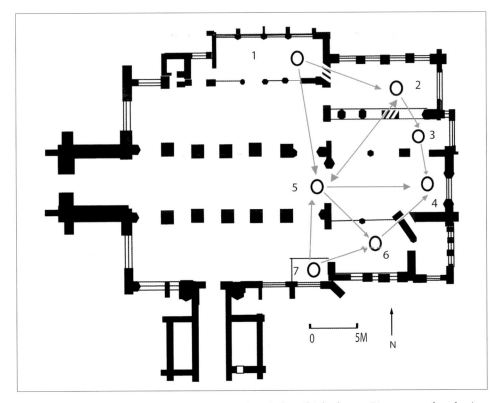

71 Conjectured visual relationships between chapel altars/high altar at Cirencester church: 1) Holy Trinity chapel 2) Lady chapel 3) St Catherine's chapel 4) high altar 5) nave altar 6) St John the Baptist chapel 7) St Edmund's (Garstang) chapel

gave a view to the high altar. The first squint provided a view to the south chapel only, suggesting in this case a possible order of precedence or 'spiritual hierarchy' between subsidiary altars, as well as the high altar. Here the celebrant in the north chapel could clearly see the priest serving the nave or south transept altar, but could not be viewed in return due to the narrowness of the squint. This may suggest that it was not necessary for the other priests to see the elevation at the mass carried out in the north chapel. Similarly, the squint at St James's in Taunton provided a view, not to the high altar but to the south chapel, or alternatively a rood altar, suggesting an order of precedence between these two, with the south chapel altar taking priority. A similar arrangement can be seen at Bradford-on-Avon (72). What is significant about all these examples is that in many cases, recorded chantry chapels were required to have a view of either the high altar or unrecorded or unspecified subsidiary altars. It is tempting to consider here whether or not there was a requirement for many lay-founded altars to have a view of 'official' church altars, which would further suggest that the latter had precedence. More research needs to be done on this subject, but nonetheless it is interesting to conjecture the nature of such relationships. Certainly the evidence gathered so far is indicative of the types of information that can be extracted from church fabric by a primarily archaeological approach.

The analysis of aspects of chantry chapel space and location, then, reveals the direct role chantry chapels played in communal religion. In many cases they were not separate entities, but linked into a wider ritual network. It also implies that many chantries and chapels were highly inclusive components in a complex

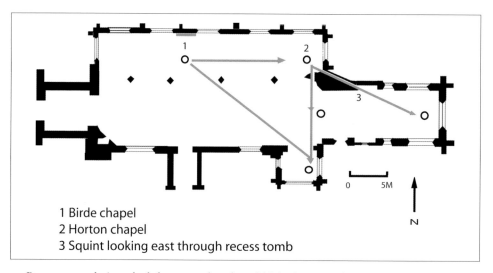

1 Birde chapel
2 Horton chapel
3 Squint looking east through recess tomb

72 Reconstructed view-sheds between chapels and high altar at Holy Trinity, Bradford-on-Avon (Roffey 2007)

network of relationships within the church – particularly in the parish churches, where, arguably, communal ties were stronger and more enduring and where the bonds between the living and those that had passed away were perhaps more intimate. Importantly, the ways in which these relationships between chapels and the wider community were negotiated were far from static. At Stoke Charity, the Hampton chapel was founded as a chantry sometime in the late fifteenth century. In the early sixteenth century the chapel seems to have been subject to a change in liturgical direction, with the focus shifting from the altar at the east end to a new altar and Easter sepulchre of John Waller (d.1525) on the chapel's north wall. This change also brought about the insertion of a new window in the north wall to accentuate this new ritual space, as well as the insertion of the double squint which permitted the parishioners to see the tomb from the nave. The squint may have also enabled people in the north aisle to see the chancel. These alterations alert us to the changing ritual nature of the chapel. Importantly, it also suggests that communal visual accessibility was the priority and determined a series of changes within chapel ritual geography, which in turn reaffirms that the public were meant to have a relationship with such monuments.

In conclusion, it appears that chantry chapel location was of prime importance to the various founders and that it was largely reliant on spatial or visual requirements. Overall this analysis indicates the level of independence that founders had, not only in the design of their monuments, but also in personal beliefs in the afterlife and the related strategies for intercession that dictated such requirements. In the parish churches, where communal ties were strong, chantry chapels were often part of an inclusive network. Those chapels that were founded closer to the chancels were still interlinked visually with other areas of the church and visibility was often facilitated by the presence of squints. In comparison, chantry chapels founded in the monasteries appear to have been more exclusive and were often highly impressive monuments, relying in many cases not on the prayers of the laity but those of the 'professionally religious'; the choir monks and high clergy, as well as on proximity to important sacred foci. Evidence also suggests that there were attempts to tie chantry-based religious practice into the wider network of church ritual and possibly to establish an order of precedence between individual foundations and other church altars. These aspects further demonstrate the versatility and all-encompassing nature of intercessory practice in the churches and monasteries and the essential contribution that such institutions made to pre-Reformation religious practice.

Equally important was the spatial geography of the chapel itself – the placing of images and symbols in direct visual lines of sight. In particular tombs, though not essential additions to chantry chapel space, nonetheless provided a visual reminder of the founder. As well as their design and embellishment, their spatial and visual location within chapel space was highly important and it is to these that we shall now turn.

TOMBS AND MEMORIALS

In theory, it was not strictly necessary for the corpse of the founder to be installed within its chantry chapel, as the latter was perceived to be solely for the benefit of a soul long fled from its earthly frame. This being said, in practice tombs were an integral feature of many chantry chapels. It may have been deemed propitious by some founders to place their mortal remains in the immediate context of the chantry and its rituals. A particularly popular place of burial within chapels was close to the altar, a location attested to in many wills of the period. For example, at the priory of St Bartholomew's in Smithfield in 1432, Richard Gray requested burial 'afor ye trinite autre in chirche of Seynt Bartylmew'. Likewise in 1375 Roger de Barneburgh willed to be buried at the south end of the altar in the chapel of St Katherine in the nave. Work by archaeologist Chris Daniell on the burial preferences indicated by the medieval wills of Yorkshire and Nottinghamshire between 1389 and 1475 shows that the majority of the laity in these areas requested burial near an altar. This type of arrangement can be observed at Cobham church where a series of fourteenth-century brasses congregates around the high altar. 'Clusters' of tombs around altars can also be found in chantry chapels such as those at Brading, Great Brington and Curry Rivel. At Curry Rivel, the family's recess tombs were arranged against the north wall of the chapel and provided a visual backdrop to the proceedings. Proximity to an altar brought with it a physical association with the mass performed there; certainly, as we have seen, from the thirteenth century onwards the mass was seen as the most effective strategy for intercession. Burial close to an altar forged a connection with the mass and its implicit intercessory efficacy and highlighted one's tomb or memorial to those participating in the mass. Such patterns are also reflected in the celebration of anniversaries (obits) and the endowment of chantry masses to be celebrated at specific altars in which the body is not necessarily present, but where the name suffices to forge the link between individual and intercessory ritual.

A broad variety of tombs and memorials can be found in medieval chantry chapels. Ledger slabs and brasses often mark the position of burials under the floor, probably the most common form of church burial in the medieval period. In the north chapel at Brympton d'Evercy, a group of ledger slabs is clustered around a central Purbeck marble ledger inscribed with a cross, perhaps marking the burial of the founder (73). In the chapels of Buckland Dinham and South Wraxall, the ledger slabs are raised several centimetres above the floor surface.

A desire to make these memorials more prominent may lie behind their arrangement; since they provided a minor obstruction, they acted as triggers of awareness. Certain chantry chapels contained large table or altar tombs which, in some instances, may have functioned as altars or desks. For example at St Bartholomew's in Smithfield in 1447, Walter Shirington requested burial in 'Waldons chappelle' on the north side of the altar in a marble tomb adjoining the wall, of the length of 'two paulesfete for men to kneel and lene upon the tombe for to here masse'. Many of these tombs were decorated with secular and religious motifs. At Ilminster, for example, the tomb altar of William Wadham in the north chapel is highly elaborate, decorated with crocketed niches and the figures of Christ in Majesty surrounded by donors. Here, the use of decorative symbolism reinforced the link between such individuals, the tomb and Christ and the saints as saviour and intercessors. The size and location of the tomb, as well as the presence of a step, may also suggest that it was used as a prayer desk or table for the display of liturgical objects (*74*). The Oglander tomb at Brading is decorated with depictions of charitable acts on its north side, which looks toward the nave. Its south elevation, which faces toward the Oglander chapel, is decorated with representations of family members. A particularly impressive example is that of Alice, Duchess de la Pole, in the chapel of St John at Ewelme. The alabaster effigy of the duchess is framed by a decorated rectangular opening

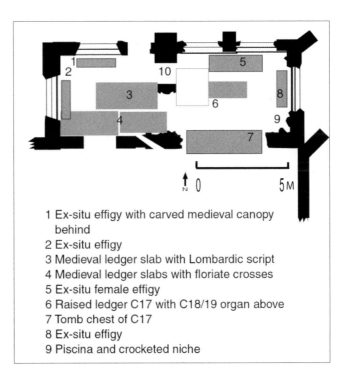

1 Ex-situ effigy with carved medieval canopy behind
2 Ex-situ effigy
3 Medieval ledger slab with Lombardic script
4 Medieval ledger slabs with floriate crosses
5 Ex-situ female effigy
6 Raised ledger C17 with C18/19 organ above
7 Tomb chest of C17
8 Ex-situ effigy
9 Piscina and crocketed niche

73 Plan of north chapel at Brympton d'Evercy church showing cluster of memorials slabs and tombs

74 Tomb altar in Wadham chapel, Ilminster church

adorned with angels and the images of saints standing on pinnacles (*75*). The tomb itself is adorned with mourners while a cadaver memorial of the duchess can be viewed through small iron grills at the foot of the tomb. At Paignton, the Kirkham chapel in the south transept is divided by a screen with two wide-arched openings within which are large tomb chests and a central opening. Two effigies sit upon each tomb chest. All three openings are fan-vaulted with pendants and crowning pinnacles with angels. There are carved images of various saints on the tombs and door surrounds. A particularly remarkable and enigmatic architectural feature is the Babington monument of *c.*1535 in the chantry chapel of John Babington at Kingston-on-Soar parish church (*colour plate 17*). The monument, which sits in the arch through to the chancel, is elaborately carved with secular and religious symbols. Originally the monument was surmounted by carved panels, now displayed on the west wall, which reached up to the ceiling. The monument was clearly devised to house a tomb, referred to in the will of Babington's wife Katherine, but this is now either lost or – more likely – was never actually constructed.

Many elaborate memorials were designed and installed to evoke memory and supplication and to function as a perpetual symbol of the individual in his or her chapel. Many of these tombs were thus visually impressive and eye-catching and displayed a synthesis of decorative, religious and secular motifs. Although there were precursors of the effigy tomb in the twelfth century, such as that of Abbot Gilbert Crispin at Westminster (1117) and Bishop Roger at Salisbury (1139), there was no real attempt to provide a true, life-like and three-dimensional portrayal.

75 Ewelme church. Effigy monument of Alice, Duchess of Suffolk, with a view through to south chapel

By the thirteenth century, as result of the growing doctrinal certainty regarding purgatory, such tombs began to depict more realistic and life-size effigies, accurately representing the physical features and clothing of the deceased, whose hands were often joined together in eternal pious prayer. At St Mary's in Warwick, the effigy tomb of Richard Beauchamp (d.1439) consists of an armoured gilt-bronze effigy on a Purbeck marble tomb chest (*colour plate 25*). The detail of the work stands out in particular on the head and hands of the effigy, where the engorged veins stand out as if the Earl is grimly concentrating his prayers heavenwards. Unusually, the hands are half-closed in what seems to be a gesture of timeless adoration. Over the tomb is a hooped frame, and around it are fourteen gilt-bronze mourners. It is one of the finest surviving medieval monuments in England. For such tombs a range of expensive materials were often used, including alabaster and brass, and in some cases they were painted. They made a statement of social standing, but more importantly they gave a salvific dimension to mortuary practice. In this sense they appropriated church space and symbolically 'presenced' the individual within it and the rituals that were enacted within it. They were used to provoke memory and prayer and were an important strategy for intercession.

Effigy tombs contained either a realistic or an idealised life-size representation of the entombed individual and were often visually impressive. These types of tomb were an attempt to provide a visual reminder of the deceased in the context of the religious practices associated with the chapels. Where they survive, they often have a central position in chantry chapel space, such as the freestanding alabaster tombs at Yatton, the large tomb of Henry Vernon and wife, replete with effigies, and the table tomb decorated with mourners at St Bartholomew's in Tong. Some, however, such as the early sixteenth-century tomb of John Leigh in the chancel at Godshill, do not occupy their chantries, but are in the chancel or naves of churches. Clearly there was a desire to make such monuments visible in the context of chantry ritual, but also in a wider context of the parish church. At the collegiate foundation of Beverley Minster, for example, the tomb of Lady Eleanor Percy (*c*.1365) is sumptuously decorated with fruit, leaves, angels with musical instruments, coats of arms and symbolic beasts (*colour plate 26*). Also featured is an Angel of the Passion with cross and nails and *Fleurs de lis*. In the Fitzalan chapel at Arundel a remarkable set of tombs survives. Perhaps the most impressive is that of Thomas Fitzalan and his wife Countess Beatrice (*c*.1415), with recumbent effigies resting on an alabaster slab with a Purbeck marble base. On the west side of the tomb, which was originally painted and gilded, are decorated gothic canopies, each of which includes a small niche where an image once resided. The niches faced the collegiate priests in the choir. Twenty-eight weepers, representing the choir monks, are lined up around the tomb, displaying opened books. Around the tomb is an iron fence with ten spikes for candles which, when lit, added a certain dramatic atmosphere to the rituals as well as drawing attention to them (*colour plate 8*). The decoration of the tombs therefore provided symbols of both a political and familial nature, juxtaposed with religious imagery, thus forging a connection between the status of the individuals and their perceived piety. Spatially, its position is important as it is in the centre of the chapel, just west of the altar steps. Naturally, the religious decoration of such tombs is often linked in particular to intercessory themes, such as the Passion and the *Fleur de lis* symbol of the Virgin Mary on the Percy tomb at Beverley. Figural depictions of mourners and weepers were a popular inclusion in the decoration of some tombs, as at Arundel and Warwick. The effigy of Bishop William Wykeham in his chantry at Winchester Cathedral has three carved human figures depicted on the soles of its feet. These probably represent the individuals responsible for the construction of the chapel and as such make an intriguing connection with the chapel building and the sole or 'soul' of the Bishop. At Cartmel Priory, the Harrington tomb (*c.*1347) is decorated with poor bedesmen, alluding to the charitable acts associated with the deceased. At Tewkesbury Abbey, the Holy Trinity chapel (*c.*1375) featured a life-size effigy of the founder, Edward Despenser. However, the effigy of Despenser is not displayed supine, but upright and kneeling, rising up above the parapets of the chapel, hands held in prayer and facing the high altar (*76*). Here, the effigy acted as a powerful *aide-mémoire* as well as giving the impression of eternal piety. The chapel also has a wall painting featuring kneeling figures of Edward and Lady Elizabeth, placing them in a context of a depiction of the Holy Trinity and angels.

The design and decoration of some tombs were also devised to publicise the specific lifetime achievements of the deceased. At Southwark Priory, the tomb of the English poet John Gower, which once stood within his chantry chapel, featured an effigy attired in a long gown and collar with a chain of interlinked 'S's, fastened with a chained swan device beneath twin portcullises to demonstrate the poet's affiliation to the Royal Court of Richard II. The head rests on the three folio volumes of Gower's principal works, *Vox Clamantis*, *Speculum Meditantis* and *Confessio Amantis*. The edge of the tomb is inscribed with a commemoration, part of which records the fact that Gower was *sacro edificio benefactor*, which may refer to his patronage of the priory church, or possibly the endowment of his chantry.

Many medieval testators in the medieval period specified in their wills that they wanted their tombs to also function as Easter sepulchres. For example, John Bobbe of Horsmonden (1484) requested that 'a tomb must be built, and on that tomb I want the sepulchre of the Lord to be set up'. Easter sepulchres were monuments that were often situated to the north of the chancel or in north chapels, the north having a special association with death and resurrection

76 Despenser chantry chapel and effigy at Tewkesbury Abbey

throughout the medieval period. Specifically, they were used during Easter week for the symbolic re-enactment of the placement of Christ in his tomb and the resurrection. The body of Christ was naturally represented by the Eucharist and hence, during Easter week, Easter sepulchres were the subject of intensive devotional practice and received much pious attention. The combination of Easter sepulchre and tomb was therefore seen as a particularly spiritually efficacious strategy as it forged a link with Eucharistic practice as well as the historically re-enacted Passion of Christ. Although many Easter sepulchres may have been temporary wooden structures, such as the 'box frame draped with cloths' referred to in the churchwardens' accounts at All Saints in Bristol, some were more permanent.

Easter sepulchres were a feature of many parish churches, yet we know very little about their use in practice. However, one rare account survives, that of Roger Martin of Long Melford, which informs us that a wooden Easter sepulchre was set up, with a frame of lighted candles on the tomb, between the Clopton chantry chapel and the chancel:

> … the sepulchre being always placed, and finely garnished, at the north end of the high altar between that and Mr Clopton's little chapel there, in a vacant place of the wall, I think upon a tomb of one of his ancestors lies between the chances and a chapel, and has a flat top surface – the Easter Sepulchre was placed on this.

The presence of what may have been an elaborately decorated Easter sepulchre was integral to the construction of the north aisle at Bradford-on-Avon for the Birde and Horton chantries. Many chapel tombs were also used as Easter sepulchres, such as the Clopton example. At Stoke Charity, the Easter sepulchre and tomb of John Waller was set up on the north wall of the Hampton chapel in the early sixteenth century (*77*). At this time a squint was also inserted to provide the laity with a view of this important ritual focus.

In most cases, Easter sepulchres were covered during Easter week. The churchwardens' accounts from All Saints refer to iron 'riddels' which may have been used for altar or wall hangings. At Stoke Charity, a large iron hook associated with the Waller canopied altar tomb on the north wall may suggest a similar fitting for the hanging of a cloth over this monument when used as an Easter sepulchre during Holy Week. In the north chapel at Portbury church there is, unusually, no east window. However, the presence of an elaborate north window may suggest a former architectural emphasis in this area of the chapel. This may have been the location of an Easter sepulchre, or the 'St Helen sarcophagus' referred to in an early sixteenth-century will. One of the best surviving examples of a combined Easter sepulchre and tomb can be found on

77 Early sixteenth-century Easter sepulchre and tomb (r) of John Waller, Stoke Charity church

the north side of the choir at Lincoln Cathedral. This decorated fourteenth-century monument contains a tomb, later ascribed to Bishop Remigius, to the west, with an Easter sepulchre to the east. Decorating the panels of the eastern portion are the defaced images of three soldiers, armed and sleeping, which represent the Roman guards present at Christ's crucifixion (*colour plate 27*).

Many of the tombs found in chantry chapels incorporated a cadaver effigy of the deceased, showing a shroud-wrapped body at an often severe stage of decomposition, such as that of Bishops Fox and Gardiner at Winchester Cathedral. Perhaps the most gruesome example is that of Abbot Wakeman at Exeter Cathedral. His cadaver tomb, at the entrance to the chapel of St Dunstan, is a depiction of the abbot's emaciated corpse riddled with various creatures and insects including a worm, snake, spider, frog and mouse. Such tombs, however, were not intended to shock, at least not in the conventional way. They were designed to act as a *memento mori* – a reminder that death could strike at any time and therefore preparation, under the guidance of mother church, should be promptly conducted. Another tomb of this type, commonly called the transi tomb, featured both the life-like recumbent effigy and a cadaver effigy, such as that of Archbishop Chichele at Canterbury. The chantry chapel of Bishop Fleming at Lincoln (*c.*1425) features a shrouded cadaver effigy below that of the attired Bishop (*colour plate 28*). Another good example is that of John, seventh Earl of Arundel, in the Fitzalan chapel at Arundel Castle (*c.*1435) (*78*). The armoured Earl is depicted in his surcoat, recumbent on top of the chest with his head reverently supported by angels. Below him the chest is pierced by three decorated 'windows' on each side. Through these windows can be seen the reality: the once fine figure of a man, embellished with his accoutrements of status and privilege reduced to the universal state, a state that all will succumb to regardless of life's achievements – a mouldering corpse. It is almost, in these cases, as if the individuals were trying to convey the idea that despite their privilege they were devout enough to realise that, unless strategies for the afterlife were practised, worldly riches amount to nothing.

We have seen the importance, in some instances, of visual accessibility to chantry chapels and their masses. Just as important, and linked to this, was the position and location of tombs. In some examples the tomb was housed within a separate area or adjunct of the chapel, as at the Clopton chapel, for example. In some of the more impressive monastic examples, on occasion the chapel was placed above the tomb and accessed by a staircase. In such cases the altar and celebrant priest were situated directly above the tomb of the deceased, forming a spatially linear association, such as the early sixteenth-century two-storey

78 Transi-tomb of John Fitzalan and Lady Chapel squint

chapel of Edmund Audley, close to the Lady Chapel at Hereford Cathedral. At Westminster Abbey, the chantry chapel of Henry V was also a two-storey arrangement with the chantry on the first floor above the effigy (*22*). Access to the chantry was via two staircases at either side of the monument. At Tewkesbury Abbey, the stone cage chapel of Richard Beauchamp (*c*.1430) had an upper storey that may have originally been the setting for the tombs of Richard and his wife Isabelle Despenser. The chosen resting place of Edward IV at St George's in Windsor was within the north choir aisle and he directed that a chantry chapel be founded in the vault immediately above it. However the King's monument was never completed, though its architectural setting survives. His will of 1475 directed that a group of almsmen were also to pray for the soul of the King and were to be provided with seats in the chantry, thus providing a 'captive' audience.

TOMBS AS 'PRESENCING MECHANISMS'

The term 'presencing mechanism', coined as we saw earlier by Pamela Graves, refers to the deliberate positioning of tombs and memorials to 'presence' themselves by visually obstructing or impinging on the rituals taking place in the church. We have seen the importance of maintaining sight-lines with the church previously, and particularly how this relates to the visual accessibility to the mass performed at various altars. The location of some tombs within such lines of sight were therefore, as Graves suggests, a powerful strategy for salvation and a means by which prayers were 'tricked' from the observing laity, or indeed the clergy. A clear example can be seen in the Fitzalan chapel in Arundel. The large decorated tomb of Thomas Fitzalan and his wife Beatrice, placed in the centre of the chapel before the podium to the high altar, visually obstructed the view of the choir priests in the stalls. As such, it acted as an obvious visual reminder, not only of patronage, but of the connection of the individuals with intercessory masses performed at the altar. It is also likely that any parishioners in the western, parish end of the chapel would have had their view of the chapel altar obstructed by the monument.

   As well as facilitating lines of sight between altars, squints could also serve to 'direct' attention to certain memorials. For example, in the former Horton chantry in the north aisle at Bradford-on-Avon, the six-metre long squint cuts through a fourteenth-century recess in the north wall of the chancel. More significantly, however, inside the squint, an inscribed memorial slab has been placed. It appears that this memorial was purposely placed to intrude itself on the priest's line of sight, and in his interaction with the high altar. It was certainly not visible to anyone else in the church and therefore appears to have been a deliberate attempt to 'presence' an individual in the Eucharistic rituals taking place. A similar arrangement can be seen at Hawton parish church, where a squint from the north chapel to the chancel cut through the recess tomb of Robert de Compton on the chancel north wall. At Yatton, the tomb of Richard Newton and wife deliberately obstructed the line of sight to the chapel altar, acting as an insistent reminder.

Another important visual location for chapel tombs was within the arcades between chapel and chancel and there are many examples of this arrangement. In the Kirkham chantry chapel at Paignton, the view from the chapel altar to the chancel high altar was 'framed' by the Kirkham monuments and acted as a visual reminder of the chapel's founders. At Minehead, the insertion of a small open recess and tomb in the wall between north chapel and chancel wall not only facilitated a visual connection between altars, but placed, or 'presenced', the individual memorial within this visual relationship. At Limington, visual access for the laity to the chapel altar is via the fourteenth-century tomb (*79*); the entombed individuals were commemorated in the context of associated Eucharistic practice. In some chapels, the tombs would have acted as a mnemonic backdrop to religious ritual, such as the fifteenth-century tomb of Emma Stafford in the decorated alcove in the north chapel at North Bradley (*80*). The motive for the placing of tombs in sight-lines between altars was to evoke the memory of the deceased, not only within the minds of the observing laity or priest, but actually within the physical sphere of the rituals observed.

This chapter has considered the various spatial and visual considerations behind chantry chapel foundation. It has revealed the level of conscious and individual planning at work behind such monuments and has shown that strategies for the medieval afterlife did not just rely on design and elaboration of chantry chapels, but also on the spatial arrangements, both internally and externally. Thus, many chantry chapels were integral components of the diverse and complex religious 'landscape' of parish and monastic churches. By the end of the Middle Ages, chapels and chantries were key components of church topography and religious practice. However, this was all to change. The Reformation of the mid-sixteenth century and the consequent dissolution of the chantries ended these complex relationships. It de-ritualised the spaces and brought a sudden end to the ecclesiastical institutions of monasteries and colleges. At a stroke, the Reformation deflated the parish, with its chantries, guilds and fraternities, as centres for communal celebration and intercessory practice. Thus the Reformation severed what had once been perceived as an eternal thread between the living and the dead, and made redundant the various strategies which served this.

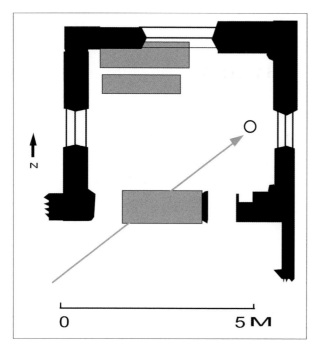

79 Reconstruction of the sight-line from the nave to the altar in the Gyvernay chapel, Limington church indicating how the tomb obstructed the former sight-line into the chapel

80 Decorated tomb recess, Stafford chapel, North Bradley

CHAPTER 8

THE REFORMATION
OF CHANTRY CHAPELS

The English Reformation of the 1530s onwards introduced a series of dramatic changes that swept away a whole tradition of devotional practice and instigated the dismantling and destruction of many religious monuments and works of art and architecture. As Eamon Duffy states, 'this was a period in which a necessity was felt to destroy, cut, hammer, scrape and melt the monuments of Catholicism into oblivion'. The performance of the mass, worship of saints, pilgrimage, prayers for the dead and beliefs in purgatory were deemed 'vain and superstitious' and consequently prohibited. Much has been lost, therefore, especially in the form of movable decorations, furnishing, fixtures and fittings. In particular the acts for the dissolution of the monasteries in the 1530s and the dissolution of the chantries in 1547 did much to obliterate the physical presence of chantry chapels, both as a political symbol of Catholic orthodoxy and as memorials dedicated to prohibited intercessory practice. As a result of the Reformation, the internal arrangements and decoration of many churches were drastically altered, screens were removed, saints' shrines dismantled and religious paintings whitewashed. The monasteries themselves were dissolved, many left ruinous and despoiled.

The Reformation was not a single event, but rather a series of events spanning the mid to late sixteenth century and stretching into the first part of the seventeenth century, with only a brief respite during the period of the Marian restoration between 1553 and 1558. Furthermore, it was foreshadowed by earlier reformist rumblings, championed in England by the Lollardist movement of the later fourteenth century. The Reformation was also far from universally popular, as many traditional historians have unjustly claimed. The progress of reformation was slow in many areas of the country, particularly in the north. However, it is certainly this period that heralded the end of the chantry, and although personal beliefs in purgatory may have been retained by some, the physical context of such beliefs, the celebration of masses and the erection of memorials dedicated to intercessory practice, were outlawed. The chantry chapel thus became a superfluous feature of the Reformation church.

In 1547, by act of Parliament, the chantry chapels were dissolved and their priests pensioned off, consigning the dead to eternal anonymity. The Chantry Act of 1547 for the dissolution of chantries and the abolition of prayers for the dead not only altered the relationship between the living and dead, but it also led to the destruction of many former chapels; their tombs, their art and their architecture. Chantries were first surveyed in 1546 in response to a statute issued by Henry VIII. As a result, commissioners in each county were required to discover and certify to the court of Augmentations the landholdings of such institutions. Henry died some months later, but his son Edward VI continued where his father had left off and by 1548, all chantries, colleges, religious brotherhoods and hospitals were surrendered to the King.

As well as the removal of the monuments themselves, the dissolution of the chantries also involved the effective dismantling of many of the institutions associated with chantry foundation, such as schools, hospitals and almshouses. For example, the school founded by Thomas Horton in 1524 at Bradford-on-Avon was out of use by 1559 and its land grants transferred to Salisbury Cathedral. During this period, many chapels where dismantled, destroyed or converted to other uses – a pattern that has largely continued to this day. Hence in today's parish churches, in particular, former chantry chapels are woefully neglected, or converted to drab functional spaces, stripped of any former decoration or furnishing.

The reformation of the chantries did not just involve the proscription of the mass, lights, obits, intercession and prayers for the dead; it also involved the physical destruction of wall paintings, sculpture and glass, and the confiscation and appropriation of related goods of value and attached land endowments. For example, at St John's in Glastonbury, the loss included silver plate, vestments, carved seats and screens and 21 chained books. At Nunney, even the iron bars of the founder's tomb were considered for appropriation. In some instances, the local reaction was to salvage artefacts before the commissioners got their hands on them. For example, at Bridgwater, everything except a lone silver chalice had been spirited away by locals beforehand. Without doubt, during the early years of the Reformation many people expected things to revert to traditional normality in due course. Therefore, many artefacts were hidden away with the expectation that they would be returned in time. In 1756, work carried out on the site of the former chantry priest's house at Wakefield, for example, revealed 25 previously hidden figures of wood and alabaster, richly ornamented with gold and vermilion. These figures apparently included a large image of St Ann teaching the young Virgin, Christ preaching, the 12 Apostles, St Paul, St John the Baptist and St William, Archbishop of York, with his pastoral staff and mitre.

Many former chantry chapels were converted for more secular purposes, such as the south chancel chantry chapel at St Michael's parish church in Southampton, which was used as a private dwelling before being pulled down some years later (*81*). At the former Augustinian priories at Smithfield and Southwark in London, the spaces of former chantry chapels were employed as blacksmiths' forges and stables respectively. At Westminster Abbey, the chantry chapel of Henry V was used as a store, while at Salisbury Cathedral the remarkable Hungerford and Beauchamp chapels at the east end of the cathedral church, were taken down as part of a general 'restoration' in the eighteenth century. At Wakefield, the bridge chantry chapel was put to a variety of secular uses, including a water store, warehouse, library, merchant's office and a cheesecake shop. In the nineteenth century, its decorated western façade was removed to nearby Kettlethorpe Hall and became the façade of a folly boathouse. At Rotherham, the bridge chapel was converted into almshouses before becoming the town jail in the eighteenth century. As at Southampton, many chapels were simply destroyed and dismantled, while the dereliction of others led to their eventual dismantling. At Mutford, the south chancel chapel was demolished in the nineteenth century, and was replaced by a brick wall with a plain window through to the chancel, in stark contrast to the overall traditional aesthetic of the building. Chantries in monasteries were normally left ruinous along with their churches. Some chapels in the cathedrals managed to survive in part, but many more were dismantled.

In many cases the spaces formerly occupied by chantries survived, but were often dramatically reorganised and ritually 'sanitised'. This form of 'spatial iconoclasm' included the removal of screens, the setting up of private pews and the insertion of large personal memorials, such as the ostentatious Wriothsley monument at Titchfield. The fact that families like the Wriothsleys, who remained staunchly Catholic, erected such monuments indicates the nature of ideological change that had affected English society at this period. At St Martin's in Stamford, the monument of Lord William Cecil (d.1598) is by far the most prominent object in that church and in its dimensions equals that of many cage chantries of the medieval period. At Stoke Charity, the Phellypes monument of around the early 1600s was placed on a podium and oriented so as to block the squint that previously provided a view from the nave to the former Easter sepulchre on the north wall of the chapel. The decades after the Reformation, then, witnessed an

81 Blocked arch to former south chantry chapel, St Michael's, Southampton

82 Medieval screen reused as a post-Reformation pew, Gaddesby church

increased emphasis on memorials dedicated to familial prestige, status and rank in life. Whereas the inscriptions of many medieval tombs exhorted prayers for the dead, now tomb inscriptions celebrated the often-embellished life of individuals and did not exhort any prayers for the soul. Naturally, this dispensed with any communal role or importance being attached to the context of chapel burial. As a result, in the parish churches in particular, the former communal importance of such chapels no longer existed. Intercessory rituals, bolstered by the prayers of the community, were not required.

Many former chantries in the parish churches became wholly private chapels or 'pews'. In some instances, such as at Cartmell Fell, Gaddesby and Whalley, pews were constructed from the screens of former chantry chapels (*82*). The period after the Reformation still witnessed the building of family chapels, such as the Knollys chapel at Rotherfield Greys, built around 1605. However, those former chantry chapels that survived were now stripped of any orthodox decoration and became more exclusive contexts for private piety, in particular family memorial and commemoration. Some chapels were now off-limits for others and detached

83 Internal view of Norreys' chapel, Rycote

visually and physically from the rest of the church, such as at Rycote, where two large enclosed wooden pews were placed in the former chantry chapel of St Michael in the late sixteenth and early seventeenth centuries. These monuments are truly impressive and clearly indicate that they were influenced by medieval cage chantry chapels. Both are canopied and enclosed by decorated screens and they completely dominate the space around the high altar (*83, colour plate 29*). The Hoare family pew at Stourton was sealed off from the nave and its interior could only be viewed by the priest in the pulpit. The former Darrell chantry at Ramsbury had a private entrance inserted into its north wall and stalls introduced for the local Popham family. Such changes forced the tearing out of a tomb from its recess and the blocking of the entrance from the north aisle to the chapel, effectively sealing off the chapel from the rest of the church. Clearly, many former chantry chapels retained their family connections and use, such as the Spencer chapel at Great Brington and the Bardolph chapel at Mapledurham. The Long chapel at South Wraxall became the Long family pew in 1566, and in the same period the Coplestone chapel at Colebroke was retained as the family chapel. The chantry of the Bretts − a family of notable recusants − at Whitestaunton survived as a family chapel with an elaborate portal entrance added in 1588. Many post-Reformation chapels were also converted to family mausoleums. At Chenies, the medieval funerary chapel built for the Russell earls of Bedford has a wide range of tombs, described by the architectural historian Nikolaus Pevsner as 'the richest single storehouse of funeral monuments in any parish church in England'. The Bedford tombs, which are divided off from the rest of the church by an iron grille, range from 1555 to 1892, demonstrating the resilience and longevity of such foundations.

During the Reformation, many former religious focal points within the churches were transformed. Significantly, in many cases, the royal coat of arms replaced roods and Doom paintings above the chancel arches to reflect royal authority over the church. In some instances the changes were ideological as well as political. At Wenhaston, the medieval depiction of the Doom was painted over with an excerpt from Romans 13:1-4, part of which stated: 'Let every soule submit him selfe unto the authorytye of the hygher powers ...' This painting, which possibly dates to the early 1550s, reflected the belief that the fate of the soul could not now be influenced by earthly strategies. At St Nicholas's in Oddington, images were removed from their niches and texts from the Bible were painted in their stead, reflecting the general belief that the Bible led the way to salvation and not idolatry and devotional ritual (*84*). At Burford, under the east window of the church and originally the site of the altar, is a sixteenth-century inscription from Tyndale's Bible translation. In some notable instances, newly erected tombs were sometimes placed so as to invalidate the space formerly used for Catholic practice. This more subtle form of iconoclasm involved at its most basic level the placing of monuments to block or appropriate former features or areas of prior ritual importance. Hence the erection of the Goddard monument in the east end south chapel at Aldbourne, for example, the area that had served as the religious focus of the chapel for centuries. More dramatically, the placing of the excessively large monument to Edward Hungerford (d.1648) and wife in the centre of the former chapel of St Anne in the church of St Leonard at Farleigh Hungerford, in a supreme act of arrogance effectively obstructed access around the chapel and therefore to the pre-Reformation family tombs, whilst drawing one's attention to the most 'important' monument (*85*).

84 Oddington church showing post-Reformation painting including Royal coat of arms over chancel arch, and biblical texts in chancel niches

A LINGERING TRADITION?

Despite the widespread changes discussed above and the abolition of the doctrine of purgatory and prayers for the dead, in some areas of Reformation England there was a certain amount of ambiguity with regard to the afterlife. Although these ambiguities were doctrinally removed by 1552, it appears that certain concessions had to be made for some form of commemoration. For centuries, notions of a penitential afterlife had been ingrained into the medieval psyche and sudden changes were perhaps psychologically difficult. The historian David

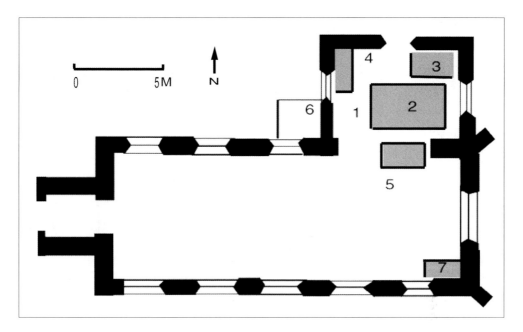

85 Arrangement of Hungerford tombs, Farleigh Hungerford: 1) chapel of St Anne 2) tomb of Edward Hungerford 1646 3) tomb of Edward Hungerford 1607 4) tomb of Mary Shaw 1613 5) tomb of Thomas and Joan Hungerford 1398/1412 6) entrance to family crypt 7) tomb of Walter and Edward Hungerford 1596/83

Loades asserts that such concessions, at a popular level, were 'extra-liturgical' and were 'tolerated rather than countenanced by the church'. Commemorating the life and achievements of the deceased, it seems, satisfied the social and psychological needs that had formerly been satisfied by the rituals of intercession. It appears that this ambiguity concerning the fate of the dead carried on into the brief period of the Marian restoration between 1553 and 1558. For example, at St Bartholomew's in Smithfield, John Garatt in 1556 bequeathed 12s to the Dominican friars (who had re-occupied the former Augustinian house) to keep a yearly dirige and a masse of requiem to be celebrated on the anniversary of his death. He also requested them to pray for his soul and those of his father, mother and two wives. At Bradford-on Avon, the school founded by Thomas Horton in 1524 remained operational for a short time. Here, the chantry priest, William Furbner, was still giving instruction in religious doctrine and training choristers as late as 1549. It cannot be ascertained if, like the foundation of new monastic houses, this period would have allowed for the eventual refoundation of chantries had the Catholic restoration proven more resilient, but it is likely. Certainly there may have been some intention to refound the Phelips chantry at Montacute, as well as the Cluniac priory there.

86 Post-Reformation tombs, south chapel, Old Basing

At parish level, this uncertainty may be more obvious. At Old Basing, the south Paulet chapel has all the features one would expect of a pre-Reformation chantry, including an altar squint. The tombs, however, somewhat enigmatically, date from the post-Reformation period (*86*). Another interesting example is the Brydges south chapel at St James in Ludgershall. The former chapel, originally dating from the fifteenth century, was refounded and rebuilt as a chapel for the tomb of Richard Brydges (d.1558), knighted during the coronation of Mary and made Sheriff of Berkshire in 1555 (*87*). The chapel provided no view to the chancel, so it is likely that it had a liturgical focus of its own, particularly in the light of the obvious Catholicism of its patron. It is likely that an altar was re-erected on the east wall, where the fifteenth-century piscina survives. It would go too far of course to claim this structure as a chantry, but it is likely that any mass said there had some connection to the deceased, whose tomb, complete with hovering angel and heraldic devices, is situated within the arch on the south side in a direct visual line between the nave and possible chapel altar. Whether or not any mass was actually celebrated in the chapel is unknown. Brydges died in 1558, the same year as his queen, and the following year the Elizabethan settlement outlawed altars and ordered their replacement with communion tables, as the Reformation recommenced.

87 Ludgershall church. Brydges tomb and chapel, seen from the nave

POST–SCRIPT: A REVIVAL OF TRADITION

The nineteenth century witnessed a revival of ritualism in the Anglican Church, which since the Reformation had stuck clearly to its Protestant values. In particular the Oxford Movement worked tirelessly to promote the reintroduction of a more emotive element to contemporary religious practice, as exemplified by the highly ritualised practices of the medieval period and supported by the iconographic interiors of the churches. In short, it sought to recover the original Catholic heritage of the Church of England. Perhaps the one building that exemplified the High Church Movement was Keble College, Oxford. The College was founded in memory of John Keble (1792-1866) a founding member of the Oxford Movement. Designed by William Butterfield and based on medieval collegiate design, Keble College consisted of a large open cloister with associated buildings centred around the large neo-Gothic chapel. Inside, the chapel was sumptuously decorated with sculptures, images, furniture and wall paintings. Though not popular in many quarters, the High Church Movement, as exemplified by Keble, was a major influence on many churches of the nineteenth century. Many parish churches were (re-)furnished with stained glass, images and wall paintings. At Highnam, the chancel art was painted with a florid depiction of the Day of Judgment, a painting found in similar contexts in the medieval period. At Asthall the chancel of the church was redecorated in Gothic style (*88*). Indeed, during this period, 'chantry chapels' were being constructed most notably by A.W. Pugin in his chapel at Ramsgate and in St George's, Southwark. However, these may have been more romantic anachronisms, than fully functioning endowments. A century or so earlier, a chapel was constructed in the church at Boxted in imitation of a pre-Reformation chantry chapel.

The High Church Movement was also to influence mortuary chapels of the period. For example, the Bateman Mausoleum at Morley was constructed in 1897 and designed as a medieval chantry chapel, making it a unique anachronism. The structure is independent but was built into part of the medieval church wall. The chapel is suitably furnished with sculpture and stained glass. At its centre is the tomb of Hugh Alleyn Sacheverell Bateman. The cross on the tomb chest was set with small crystal inserts through which the coffin may be seen. Despite all appearances, however, this was not a 'working' chantry. Some five years later though, at Westminster Cathedral, a chantry was founded for the soul of the deceased Archbishop Herbert Vaughan, a foundation which continues to this day. Today many associated buildings and areas of former

88 The chancel of Asthall church showing nineteenth-century wall paintings

89 The former chantry priest's house, Frome, now an electrical appliance shop

chantry land endowments retain a connection to their former associations and this often survives in the form of place-name evidence, such as Suffolk's largest housing estate, the Chantry, in Ipswich and the former chantry priest's house at Frome now an electrical appliance shop aptly named 'Chantry TV' (*89*). Thus, although physically long disappeared, the memory of the medieval chantry chapel is still subtly present.

CHAPTER 9

CONCLUSIONS

Despite the destructive effects of the Reformation and ensuing centuries, much structural evidence survives for the medieval chantry chapel. In some cases, this can also be related to surviving contemporary documents. Such combined evidence allows for the reconstruction of the form and fabric of medieval chantry chapels, and their specific spatial arrangements and relationships. This then provides an insight into how they were used as medieval strategies for the afterlife, and brings to light their pivotal role in private and public religious experience. The analysis of extant examples indicates that many chantry founders had, to an extent, an element of personal control and preference in the design and location of their chapels. These factors further suggest that individuals often had their own particular opinions on what made an effective strategy for the afterlife. To some, proximity to an altar or to a shrine was of prime importance. To others, public visibility or relative exclusivity were major factors. In many examples, architectural decoration, the spatial setting of chapels and the ordering of internal features such as tombs, were devised to evoke and perpetuate memory through time, to be associated with Eucharistic practices and to attract the prayers of others.

The various forms of chantry chapel foundation attest to the diversity in such institutions. A wide range of chantry chapels can be found; in churches and monasteries, hospitals, bridges, private households, gatehouses and in the guise of individual chapels, guilds and fraternities. For the wealthiest, great chantries or collegiate chapels were founded as privatised monastic institutions, often housing satellite foundations. For several years, some studies – mainly historical – of popular religion within pre-Reformation England have argued that religious practice in medieval churches became increasingly privatised as a result of the foundation of chapels and chantries. More recently, in reaction to traditional interpretations, some historians have attempted to redress the balance, in particular showing the broad and comprehensive appeal of late medieval popular Catholicism. Archaeological analysis of medieval chantry chapels, as presented by this book, further supports the assumption that chapels and chantries operated in a much wider social and religious context than previously thought. In monasteries and cathedrals, chantry chapels were often located in highly visible areas. Furthermore, though many of these examples were 'cage' chantries, completely screened, more often than not, provision was made for wider visual participation in the rituals enacted within their spaces. In parish churches, chantries were a mixture of individual and communal motives, which was typical of the medieval period. In many examples, a broad variety of concerns reveals themselves. The construction and spatial arrangement of chantry chapels only really worked on a corporate and inclusive basis.

One essential conclusion of this research is that it reveals that there were substantial changes to the churches of the medieval period as a direct consequence of chantry chapel foundation and earlier, related memorial practices. In the late medieval period we see that there arose a complex network of interactions and visual relationships within church space. Such arrangements were facilitated by the use of squints, the ordering of tombs and altars and the use of devotional architecture. Thus the sacred areas of the church were frequently linked into a common and universal structure which further bonded the community in its religious practices. Chantry chapels founded in churches and religious houses could either rely on proximity to saintly relics, the high altar or public awareness, or on the especial spiritual vitality of a community dedicated to a life of prayer, or both. These various strategies for intercession often facilitated a bond between the individual and the church or monastic community. One of the most important media for the relationship between chantry chapels and the community was vision. In most cases, it was a priority to ensure that the mass performed within the chapel was made visible to the wider community. Often, these important lines of sight were manipulated to incorporate the presence of memorials and intercessory triggers. Furthermore, there appears to be evidence to suggest that efforts were made to 'tie' the chantry masses into a general 'network' of rituals performed throughout the church, such as those celebrated within other chapels and especially at the high altar. This research therefore strongly suggests that in many instances there was a visual relationship between subsidiary altars, while others can be inferred and conjectured. Consequently, the evidence presented suggests the extent to which chantries and chapels were very much part of their churches.

The overall implication of these conclusions is significant. The question is raised as to whether such developments occurred by accident, as a result of 'fashion', or were a direct consequence of a coordinated policy. Such motives, whether influenced by a desire for religious innovation or a further context for private piety, were probably instigated by the greater monasteries and later colleges, and may have filtered down to parish level under the influence of the gentry and mercantile classes. Significantly, as this research has shown, such influences were not just confined to the wealthy urban churches, but are found in rural examples also. Here we see the ruling classes using their parish churches for personalised intercession and the encouragement of associated corporate response. Thus, it may be argued, such a movement transported a wide range of forms of religious practice out of the confines of the monasteries and colleges into the wider community.

In conclusion, this book has provided an archaeological investigation into the nature of medieval chantry chapels, drawn from a range of specific examples, and an examination of their role as strategies for the medieval afterlife. It has highlighted the spatial and visual relationships between the chapels and the rest of the church and its community, and the wider social role of chantry foundations. It has not been the intention to examine the social and economic history of chantry chapels, or to provide a comprehensive survey of the various forms of foundation – or even to discuss in any detail non-perpetual chantries – but to investigate the physical forms and components of specific chantry chapels and how they operated as strategies for the afterlife. This work has illustrated that, a few notable examples aside, medieval chantry chapels were not 'stand-alone' monuments. They interrelated with other areas and monuments within the church, and often depended upon forming an associative relationship with these. This study has illustrated that the late medieval chantry chapel was a vital and integral component of medieval religion, and that it evolved out of a series of related practices and monuments as early as the late Anglo-Saxon period. Chantry foundations made a major and wide-ranging contribution to late medieval society, and many were of great significance to the lives of ordinary people. Chantry chapels were versatile and influential monuments, repositories of works of art and architecture of the highest order, and an important feature of medieval cultural heritage – a heritage that is now all but vanished.

SELECT BIBLIOGRAPHY
AND FURTHER READING

Allen, W. (1565, re-edited 1886) *A Defense and Declaration of the Catholike Churches Doctrine touching Purgatory, and Prayers of the Soules Departed* Antwerp

Ariès, P. (1974) *Western Attitudes Toward Death: From the Middle Ages to the Present* Baltimore: John Hopkins University Press

Ariès, P. (1981) *The Hour of Our Death* trans. H. Weaver, Harmondsworth: Penguin

Bainbridge, V.R. (1994) 'The Medieval Way of Death: Commemoration and the After-life in Pre-Reformation Cambridgeshire' in Wilks, M. (ed.), *Prophecy and Eschatology* Studies in Church History Subsidia 10, 183-204

Beresford, M. and Hurst, J. (1990) *Wharram Percy* London: English Heritage

Binski, P. (1996) *Medieval Death: Ritual and Representation* London: British Museum Press

Blair, J. (2005) *The Church in Anglo-Saxon Society* Oxford: Oxford University Press

Boddington, A., Cadman, G. and Cramp, R. (1996) *Raunds Furnells: The Anglo-Saxon Church and Churchyard* English Heritage Research Report 7

Bond, C.J. (1988) 'Church and Parish in Norman Worcestershire' in Blair, J. (ed.) *Minsters and Parish Churches: the Local Church in Transition 950–1200,* Oxford: Oxford University Committee for Archaeology 17, 119-35

Bossy, J. (1983) 'The Mass as a Social Institution 1200-1700' *Past and Present* 100, 29-61

Brown, S. (1999) *Sumptuous and Richly Adorn'd: The Decoration of Salisbury Cathedral* London HMSO: RCHME

Burgess, C.R. (1988) 'A Fond Thing Vainly Invented: An Essay on Purgatory and Pious Motive in Later Medieval England' in Wright, S.J. (ed.) *Parish Church and People: Local Studies in Lay Religion 1350–1750* London: Hutchinson, 56-85

Burgess, C.R. (1996) 'St Mary-at-Hill, London' in Blair, J. and Golding, B. (eds), *The Cloister and the World: Essays in Medieval History in Honour of Barbara Harvey* Oxford: Clarendon Press, 247-72

Burgess, C.R. (2000) *The Pre-Reformation Records of All Saints', Bristol, Part 1* Bristol: Bristol Record Society Publication, vol. 53

Burgess, C.R. (2000) '"Longing to be Prayed For": Death and Commemoration in an English Parish in the later Middle Ages' in Gordon, B. and Marshall, P. (eds.) *The Place of the Dead: Death and Remembrance in Late Medieval and Early Modern Europe* Cambridge: Cambridge University Press, 44-65

Burgess, C.R. (2004) *The Pre-Reformation Records of All Saints', Bristol, Part 2* Bristol: Bristol Record Society Publication, vol. 56

Burgess, C.R. (2005) 'St George's College, Windsor: Context and Consequence' in Saul, N., 63-97

Colgrave, B. & Mynors, R.A.B. (1969) *Bede's Ecclesiastical History of the English Church and People* London: Penguin

Colvin, H.M. (1991) *Architecture and Afterlife* London: Yale University Press

Colvin, H.M. (2000) 'The Origin of Chantries' *Journal of Medieval History* 26, 163-73

Cook, G.H. (1947) *Medieval Chantries and Chantry Chapels* London: Phoenix

Cook, G.H. (1958) *English Collegiate Churches* London: Phoenix

Crouch, D. (2000) *Piety, Fraternity and Power: Religious Guilds in Late Medieval Yorkshire, 1389-1547* Woodbridge: Boydell and Brewer

Crouch, D. (2001) 'The Origin of Chantries: Some Further Anglo-Norman Evidence' *Journal of Medieval History* 27, 159-80

Daniell, C. (1996) 'When Penance Continued in the Grave' *British Archaeology* 19

Daniell, C. (1997) *Death and Burial in Medieval England 1066-1550* London: Routledge

Daniell, C. and Thompson, V. (1999) 'Pagans and Christians' in Jupp, P. & Gittings, C. (eds), *Death in England: An Illustrated History* Manchester: Manchester University Press, 65-90

Daunton, C., *The iconography and patronage of medieval stained glass in Norfolk* University of East Anglia M.Phil, in progress

Dobson, R.B. (ed.) (1984) *The Church, Patronage and Politics in the Fifteenth Century* Gloucester: Alan Sutton

Duffy, E. (1992) *The Stripping of the Altars. Traditional Religion in England 1400-1580* London: Yale University Press

Edwards, K. (1967) *The English Secular Cathedrals in the Middle Ages* Manchester: Manchester University Press

Egan, G. (Oct. 2002) 'Hopeful Dead Clutching their Tickets to Heaven' *British Archaeology* 67

Farnhill K. (2001) *Guilds and the Parish Community in Late Medieval East Anglia, c.1470-1550* York: York Medieval Press

Finch, J. (2000) *Church Monuments in Norfolk before 1850* Oxford: BAR British Series 317

French, K.L. (2001) *The People of the Parish: Community Life in a Late Medieval English Diocese* Philadelphia: University of Pennsylvania

French, K.L., Gibbs, G. G. and Kumin, B. (eds), (1997) *The Parish in English Life 1400-1600* Manchester: Manchester University Press

Gibb, J.H.P. (1976) 'The Anglo-Saxon Cathedral at Sherborne' *Archaeological Journal* 132, 71-111

Goodall, J.A.A. (2001) *God's House at Ewelme. Life, Devotion and Architecture in a Fifteenth-Century Almshouse* London: Ashgate Press

Graves, C.P. (2000) *Form and Fabric of Belief: The Archaeology of Lay Experience in Medieval Norfolk and Devon* Oxford: BAR British Series 311

Green, E. (2002) 'Bridge Chapels' *Historic Churches* Historic Churches Preservation Trust

Hadley, D.M. (2001) *Death in Medieval England* Stroud: Tempus

Heighway, C. and Bryant, R. (1999) *The Golden Minster: The Anglo-Saxon Minster and Later Medieval Priory of St Oswald's, Gloucester* York: CBA Research Report British Series 117

Hicks, M. (1987) 'The Piety of Margaret, Lady Hungerford (d.1478)' *Journal of Ecclesiastical History* vol. 38 no. 1, 19-39

Hines, J., Cohen, N. and Roffey, S. (2004) 'Iohannes Gower, Armiger, Poeta: Records and Memorials of his Life and Death' in Echard, S. (ed.), *A Gower Companion* Cambridge: D.S. Brewer, 1-41

Klukas, A.W. (1984) 'Liturgy and Architecture: Deerhurst Priory as an Expression of Regularis Concordia' *Viator* 15, 81-106

Kreider, A. (1979) *English Chantries: The Road to Dissolution* London: Harvard University Press

Kumin, B. (1996) *The Shaping of a Community: The Rise and Reformation of the English Parish, c.1400-1560* Aldershot: Scholar Press

Loades, D. (1994) 'Rites of Passage and the Prayer Books of 1549 and 1552', in Wilks, M. (ed.), *Prophecy and Eschatology* Studies in Church History Subsidia 10, 205-16

Le Goff, J. (1984) *The Birth of Purgatory* trans. A. Goldhammer, Aldershot: Scolar Press

Lindley, P. (2002) *Image and Idol: Medieval Sculpture* (Video Presentation) Illuminations

Morris, R. (1989) *Churches in the Landscape* London: Phoenix

Rahtz, P. and Watts, L. (1997) *St Mary's Church, Deerhurst, Gloucestershire* London: Phillimore

Reynolds, A. (1993) 'A Survey of the Parish church of St Swithin at Compton Bassett, Wiltshire' *Wiltshire Archaeological Magazine* 86, 102-112

Reynolds, A. (1999) *Later Anglo-Saxon England: Life and Landscape* Stroud: Tempus

Reynolds, A. & Turner, S. (2005) 'Discovery of a late Anglo-Saxon monastic site in Devon: Holy Trinity church, Buckfastleigh', *Archaeology International* 2004/5 (8), 22-25

Richmond, C. & Scarff, E. (eds), (2001) *St George's Chapel, Windsor, in the Late Middle Ages* Windsor: Dean and Canons of Windsor

Rodwell, W. & Rodwell, K. (1982) 'St Peter's Church, Barton-upon-Humber: Excavation and Structural Study, 1978-81', *Antiquaries Journal* 62, 283-315

Roffey, S. (2003) 'Deconstructing a Symbolic World: The Reformation and the English Medieval Parish Chantry' in Gaimster, D. and Gilchrist, R. (eds), *The Archaeology of Reformation* Society for Post-Medieval Archaeology Monograph 1, London: Maney, 342-55

Roffey, S. (2006) 'Constructing a Vision of Salvation: Chantries and the Social Dimension of Religious Experience in the Medieval Parish Church' *Archaeological Journal* 163, 122-146

Roffey, S. (2007) *The Medieval Chantry Chapel: An Archaeology* Woodbridge: Boydell Press

Saul, N. (ed.), (2005) *St Georges Chapel, Windsor, in the Fourteenth Century* Woodbridge: Boydell

Scarisbrick, J. (1984) *The Reformation and the English People* Oxford: Clarendon Press

Southern, R.W. (1982) 'Between Heaven and Hell' in *The Times Literary Supplement* 18 June, 651-52

Symons, T. (1951) *Regularis Concordia* London: Thomas Nelson and Sons

Thomson, J.A.F. (1983) *The Transformation of Medieval England 1370-1529* London: Longmans

VCH (1909) Victoria County History of London Vol.1, London

Weaver, F.W. (1905) *Somerset Medieval Wills, 1531-1558* Somerset Record Society 21

Weaver, F.W. (1903) *Somerset Medieval Wills, 1501-1530* Somerset Record Society 19

Weaver, F.W. (1901) *Somerset Medieval Wills, 1383-1500* Somerset Record Society 16

Webb, E. (1921) The Records of St Bartholomew's Priory and St Bartholomew the Great, West Smithfield Vols 1 & 2, London

Westlake, H.F. (1919) *The Parish Guilds of Medieval England* London and New York: S.P.C.K

Whitelock, D. (1955) *English Historical Documents c. 500- 1042* London: Meuthen

Wood-Legh, K.L. (1965) *Perpetual Chantries in Britain* Cambridge: Cambridge University Press

Yorke, B. (forthcoming) 'The Burial of Kings in Anglo-Saxon England' in Owen-Crocker, G. (ed.), *Royal Authority* Woodbridge: Boydell and Brewer

GENERAL INDEX

Aisle
  and the parish church 46-7
  and the public 29, 134-6
  function of 45-9
  processional 132
Altar
  and burial 53-4, 154-63, 181
  and Reformation 176
  and visual relationships 20, 27, 28,
    39, 47, 95, 113, 134-54, 163-66, 176,
    182
  high 128-31
Anchorite/anchoress 92
  cell 103
Ars Moriendi 55
Athanasian creed 52
Augustinian order 45, 62, 63, 64, 121,
  169, 175
Bede 34, 55
Benedictine order 66, 84, 128
Bible, Tyndale's 173
Bishops 26, 63, 70
  Arch- 37, 54, 72, 82, 86, 105, 125,
    162, 169, 178
  Aethelwold, of Winchester 34, 35, 41
  Alcock, of Ely 74, 120
  Audley, of Hereford and Salisbury
    72, 120, 128
  Beauchamp, of Salisbury 68, 125
  Beaufort, of Winchester 120, 124
  Brantyngham, of Exeter 120
  Braybrook, of St Paul's, London 65
  De Bridport, of Salisbury 74
  De Gower, of St David's,
    Pembrokeshire 77
  De la Wyle, of Salisbury 86
  Edington, of Winchester 120, 123,
    132
  Fleming, of Lincoln 125, 162
  Fox, of Winchester 70, 72, 120, 162
  Gardiner, of Winchester 77, 120,
    162
  Gifford, of Worcester 54, 128
  Gower, of St David's,
    Pembrokeshire 145
  Hatfield, of Durham 77
  Henry of Blois, of Winchester 45
  Hugh, of Wells 63
  Hungerford, of Salisbury 125
  Langley, of Durham 123
  Langton, of Winchester 69, 137

Longland, of Lincoln 125
Neville, of Durham 67
Nyke, of Norwich 122
Remigius, of Lincoln 162
Roger, of Salisbury 156
Russell, of Lincoln 125
Savage, of York 105
Stanbury, of Hereford 144-5
Vaughan, of St David's,
  Pembrokeshire 70
Wayneflete, of Winchester 120, 124
West, of Ely 77, 120
William of Wykeham, of
  Winchester 81, 120, 123, 159
Burial
  and altars 154
  and battlefields 79-80
  and the porticus 37
  Anglo-Saxon 31-3
  charcoal 53
  cloister 110
Campanile 92
Cathedrals (general; for specific
  cathedrals, see index of places) 15,
  23, 25, 27, 61, 63, 64, 65, 68, 93, 94,
  95, 107, 120, 123, 130, 132, 139, 143,
  150, 169, 182
Catholic restoration 175
Chantry
  Act 168
  certificates 26
  definition of 16, 29
  stone-cage 73, 95
  surveys 26, 168
Chapel
  almshouse 86-8
  bastion 92
  bridge 89-92, 181
  cathedral 61, 65
  collegiate 61-3, 65-6, 77-86, 181
  gatehouse 92-3, 181
  guild 106-8
  hospital 86-8, 181
  house 93-4, 181
  monastery 58, 61, 65, 181
  parish church 94-106
  wall 92
Choir 38, 61, 64, 66, 71, 72, 77, 79,
  102, 120, 121, 123, 128, 130, 134,
  144, 145, 153, 158, 162, 164
  retro- 137, 138

Chronicon Lemovicense 53
Church tower 37, 43, 92, 102, 103,
  140
Churchwardens' accounts 24, 26, 51,
  161
Cistercian order 64
Clement
  of Alexandria 12
  VI, Pope 124
Colleges 58, 61, 65, 66, 77-86, 88, 107,
  165, 168, 177, 183
Confessions 33
Council of Lyon 33, 52
Decoration
  and the Reformation 112, 167,
    168, 171
  function of 20, 41, 64, 74, 109, 110,
    119, 136, 159, 181
Dirige 21, 175
Dissolution 26, 61, 62, 165, 167, 168
Documentary sources 24, 25-6, 27, 31,
  58, 90, 92, 95
Easter sepulchre 102, 145, 153, 159,
  161, 162, 169
Enoch 33
Fourth Lateran Council 51
Fraternity 47, 63, 91, 108
Gregory the Great, Pope 34
Guilds 17, 23, 42, 43, 47, 63, 90, 92, 96,
  105, 106-8, 116, 140, 165, 181
High Church Movement 177-9
Historia Ecclesiastica 34
Homilies 34
Host, Elevation of the 19, 20, 47, 136
IHS motif/monogram 114
Images 19, 20, 27, 28, 29, 35, 54, 55, 59,
  71, 74, 99, 110, 112, 113-4, 115, 116,
  123, 153, 156, 158, 159, 162, 173,
  177, 187
Keble, John 177
Liber Vitae 35, 63
Life of St Cuthbert 34
Lily cross, Christ on the 114
Lytel Boke 52
Maccabees, II 33
Marian restoration 167, 175
Mass
  and guilds 42-3
  and intercession 19, 38, 44, 54, 57,
    59, 154
  and the Reformation 167, 168

and visual access 20, 28-9, 47, 95, 134, 136, 140, 164, 182
high 66
low 150
missae currentes 159
morrow 134
requiem 66
significance of 19, 20, 35, 66, 147
Monastic
reform 35, 41
revival 35, 44-5
Monk 34, 36, 41, 55, 62, 65, 123, 128, 132, 136, 153, 158
More, Thomas 55
Nave 16, 29, 36, 40, 57, 59, 61, 68, 70, 71, 72, 77, 79, 84, 85, 99, 105, 107, 114, 120, 121, 122, 123, 132, 134, 137, 138, 140, 145, 146, 151, 152, 153, 154, 155, 158, 166, 169, 172, 176, 177
Obit Book see *Liber Vitae*
Office for All Saints 41
Office for the Dead 41
Ordynace of Chrysten Men 52
Origen 33
Oxford Movement see High Church Movement
Piscina 47, 94, 134, 176
Placebo 21
Porticus 36-41
Priests 18 19, 26, 34, 36, 42, 44, 45, 51, 53, 62, 64, 65, 66, 72, 79, 81, 86, 87, 89, 90, 91, 99, 101, 102, 107, 131, 134, 136, 140, 144, 145, 150, 152, 158, 164, 165, 168, 169, 172, 178, 179

Purgatory 16, 19, 21, 33-6, 49, 51, 52-5, 55-9, 63, 124, 158, 167, 168, 174
Regularis Concordia 34, 35, 41
Requiem 21, 66, 175
Saints
and the Reformation 167, 168
as intercessors 16-7, 35, 74, 155
royal 113
shrines of 54, 123, 124-8, 167
St Alban 74
St Amphibal 74
St Ann 169
St Anne 66, 74
St Augustine of Hippo 34-5, 55
St Bridget of Sweden 55
St Christopher 114, 116
St Cuthbert 34, 35
St Edmund 103, 113, 116
St Edward the Confessor 54, 113
St Faith 116
St George 114
St Gregory 41, 113
St James 66
St John the Baptist 169
St Martina 116
St Olaf of Norway 113
St Osmund 125
St Oswald 54
St Oswin 74
St Patrick 55, 56
St Paul 169
St Peter 65, 66
St Swithun 124
St Thomas Becket 124

St Thomas of Canterbury 90
St Wilgefortis 85
St William 169
Screens, function of 17, 28, 38, 69, 70, 77, 120, 136-8, 171
Soul-scot 35
Symbols
and sight lines 153
religious 53, 108, 109, 110, 112, 114, 156, 159
secular 27, 43, 44, 85, 99, 104, 105, 109, 117, 159
Sedilia, definition of 137
Seven Corporal Works of Mercy 58
Shrines 27, 38, 40, 41, 52, 53, 54, 57, 85, 119, 121, 122, 123, 124-8, 132, 138, 143, 167, 181
Squint 28, 47, 72, 96, 102, 113, 131, 132, 134, 136, 138-53, 161, 163, 164, 165, 169, 176, 182
Statutes of Mortmain 25
Supplication of Souls 55
Three paths of the dead 33
Transi tomb 162
Transubstantiation 20, 47
Trental, the 21, 34, 41
Uncumber see St Wilgefortis
Valor Ecclesiasticus 26
View-shed analysis 28
Vision of Drythelm 34
Wall painting 17, 55, 57, 74, 77, 110, 113, 114-6, 159, 168, 177, 178
Wills 21, 24, 26, 57, 154, 159

INDEX OF PLACES

Aldbourne, Wiltshire 47, 140, 173
Aldsworth, Gloucestershire 95
All Cannings, Wiltshire 105
Alton Barnes, Wiltshire 43, 44
Arundel, West Sussex 43, 84, 158, 159, 162-3, 164
Ashingdon, Essex 44
Ashton, Devon 115
Asthall, Oxfordshire 134, 135, 178
Avebury, Wiltshire 132
Barton-Turf, Norfolk 113
Battlefield College Shropshire, 79
Bedwyn, Wiltshire 43
Berkeley, Gloucestershire 109
Beverley Minster, East Yorkshire 84, 107, 158
Bewdley, Worcestershire 90
Bishops Cannings, Wiltshire 47, 105
Bishops Cannings, Wiltshire 105
Bishopstone, Sussex 32, 40
Bishopstone, Wiltshire 111
Bisley-with-Lypiatt, Gloucestershire 93
Blackfriars (Dominicans), York 66
Boarhunt, Hampshire 44
Boxgrove Priory, East Sussex 144, 150
Boxted, Suffolk 178
Boyton, Wiltshire 79, 80, 86, 109
Bradford-on-Avon, Wiltshire 36, 39, 41, 140, 175
Brading, Isle of Wight 154, 155
Bray, Berkshire 95
Breamore, Hampshire 36, 37, 41
Bridgwater, Somerset 99, 105, 113, 140, 168
Bridport, Dorset 94
Bristol Abbey (Cathedral) 62, 121
Britford, Wiltshire 103
Bromham, Wiltshire 101, 108, 109, 113
Brympton d'Evercy, Somerset 140, 143, 154, 155
Buckfastleigh, Devon 37, 95, 107
Burford, Oxfordshire 95, 123, 138, 173
Bury St Edmunds, Suffolk 112
Byland Abbey, North Yorkshire 62, 64
Cambridge, Cambridgeshire 80, 81, 93
Canterbury, Kent 36, 37, 38, 41, 47, 54, 68, 86, 90, 124, 125, 162
Canterbury Cathedral, Kent 36, 38, 41, 54, 68, 124, 125, 162
Cartmel Priory, Lancashire 159

Cartmell Fell, Lancashire 171
Caversham, Berkshire 90
Cheddar, Somerset 47, 137
Chenies, Buckinghamshire 173
Cherry Hinton, Cambridgeshire 137
Chew Magna, Somerset 95
Childrey, Oxfordshire 87
Chingford, Essex 93
Chipping Norton, Oxfordshire 96, 98, 107, 123, 139, 151
Christchurch Priory, Dorset 68, 69, 72, 128, 132, 140, 141, 143, 150
Churchill, Somerset 140, 151
Cirencester, Gloucestershire 88, 96, 105, 114, 151
Cobham, Kent 154
Colaton Raleigh, Devon 93
Colchester Priory, Essex 62
Colebroke, Devon 173
Compton, Surrey 47, 103, 139
Compton Bassett, Wiltshire 69
Corhampton, Hampshire 43, 44
Corsham, Wiltshire 130
Coventry, Warwickshire 57, 91, 106, 107
Crediton, Devon 79
Crewkerne, Somerset 105, 106
Cullompton, Devon 99, 100, 103, 104, 109, 110, 111, 122, 132
Curry Rivel, Somerset 154
Deerhurst, Gloucester 36, 38, 40, 41, 42
Derby, Derbyshire 90
Devizes, Wiltshire 18, 101, 103, 108, 109, 113
Dover, Kent 36
Droitwich, Worcestershire 90
Droxford, Hampshire 113
Ducklington, Oxfordshire 109
Durham Cathedral, County Durham 67, 69, 71, 77, 121, 123, 136
Earls Barton, Northamptonshire 43
East Horndon, Essex 101
Ely Cathedral, Cambridgeshire 74, 77, 120, 123, 130
Escomb, County Durham 44
Etchingham, East Sussex 54
Evesham, Gloucestershire 110
Ewelme, Oxfordshire 23, 87, 88, 110, 114, 115, 155, 157
Exeter Cathedral, Devon 65, 74, 77, 120, 121, 123, 132, 162

Faccombe Netherton, Hampshire 44
Fairford, Gloucestershire 116
Farleigh Hungerford, Somerset 99, 114, 116, 173, 175
Fotheringhay, Northamptonshire 84
Fyfield, Berkshire 86
Gaddesby, Leicestershire 109, 113, 171
Glastonbury, Somerset 41, 168
Godshill, Isle of Wight 114, 158
Goltho, Lincolnshire 44
Gravesend, Kent 87
Great Brington, Northamptonshire 110, 120, 154, 173
Great Chalfield, Wiltshire 140
Grey Friars, Beverley, East Yorkshire 107
Greyfriars, London 66
Grundisburgh, Suffolk 103
Hambledon, Hampshire 140
Harby, Nottinghamshire 63
Hawton, Nottinghamshire 165
Hengrave Hall 116
Hereford Cathedral, Herefordshire 63, 120, 123, 145, 164
Hessett, Suffolk 102
Hexham, Northumberland 41
Heytesbury, Wiltshire 79, 86
Higham Ferrers, Northamptonshire 81
Highnam, Gloucestershire 177
Holy Trinity, Aldgate, London 62
Holy Trinity, Coventry 57, 107
Horsmonden, Kent 159
Hull, East Yorkshire 107
Ilminster, Somerset 105, 134, 135, 155, 156
Jarrow, Northumberland 37
Kellington, Lincolnshire 52
Kendal, Cumbria 98, 109
Kilve, Somerset 79
Kimpton, Bedfordshire 58
Kingston-on-Soar, Nottinghamshire 110, 112, 156
Lacock, Wiltshire 105, 110, 112
Langport, Somerset 92
Lavenham, Suffolk 96, 99, 102, 137, 138
Lechlade, Gloucestershire 91
Leicester, Leicestershire 86, 88
Limington, Somerset 165, 166
Lincoln Cathedral, Lincolnshire 63,

65, 77, 125, 126, 136, 137, 140, 145, 146, 150, 162
London Charterhouse 64
Long Melford, Suffolk 21, 101, 102, 114, 116, 140, 161
Ludgershall, Wiltshire 176, 177
Luton, Bedfordshire 95
Macclesfield, Cheshire 105
Mapledurham, Oxfordshire 173
Marwell, Hampshire 45
Minehead, Somerset 120, 165
Montacute, Somerset 101, 105, 120, 175
Morley, Derbyshire 178
Mutford, Suffolk 169
Nettlecombe, Somerset 120
Newark, Nottinghamshire 95, 96, 97, 140, 142, 151
Niton, Isle of Wight 47
North Bradley, Wiltshire 165, 166
North Elmham, Norfolk 53
North Leigh, Oxfordshire 57, 58, 110
Norwich Cathedral, Norfolk 122, 145
Nottingham, Nottinghamshire 90
Nunnaminster, Winchester 66
Nunney, Wiltshire 168
Oddington, Gloucestershire 57, 173, 174
Old Basing, Hampshire 99, 100, 109, 131, 140, 176
Old Minster, Winchester 41, 53
Outwell, Norfolk 116
Paignton, Devon 156, 165
Petham, Kent 93
Pickering, North Yorkshire 58, 114
Portbury, Wiltshire 132, 161
Portchester, Hampshire 43
Pulham, Norfolk 107
Ramsbury, Wiltshire 172
Ramsgate, Kent 178
Raunds 43, 53
Raunds Furnells, Northamptonshire 52
Reculver, Kent 36
Rochester, Kent 41, 105, 109
Rotherfield Greys, Oxfordshire 171
Rotherham, West Yorkshire 90, 92, 169
Roxton, Derbyshire 137
Rycote, Oxfordshire 172
Salisbury Cathedral, Wiltshire 61, 64, 65, 67, 68, 71, 72, 74, 75, 86, 93, 121, 123, 125, 128, 132, 147, 150, 168, 169
Scarborough, North Yorkshire 95, 105, 106

Shaftesbury, Dorset 35
Sherborne, Dorset 38
Sherston, Somerset 132, 140, 143
Snergate, Kent 95
Snettisham, Norfolk 45
Solihull, West Midlands 99
South Leigh, Oxfordshire 16, 17, 57, 114, 136, 137, 138
South Mimms, Middlesex 114
South Wraxall, Wiltshire 154, 173
Southampton, Hampshire 92, 169, 170
Southwark Priory (Cathedral), London 62
Southwell, Nottinghamshire 72
Southwold, Suffolk 113
Sowerby, North Yorkshire 140
St Alban's Abbey, Hertfordshire 72, 74, 76, 122, 125, 128
St Andrew's, Holborn, London 64, 71
St Bartholomew-the-Great, Smithfield, London 62, 63, 64, 66, 154, 155, 175
St Botolph's, Aldersgate, London 64
St Bride's, London 57, 106
St Cuthbert's, Wells, Somerset 34, 138
St David's Cathedral, Pembrokeshire 70, 77, 79, 145, 147, 148, 149
St Edmund's, Salisbury, Wiltshire 86
St George's Cathedral, Southwark 178
St Helens-on-the-Walls, York 52
St Ives, Cambridgeshire 47, 90, 92
St John's, Clerkenwell, London 64
St Mark's hospital, Bristol 88
St Martin's, Canterbury 38, 47
St Mary-at-Hill, London 51
St Mary Spital, London 54, 88
St Mary's, Warwick, Warwickshire 79, 84, 101, 116, 158
St Nicholas Shambles, London 53
St Oswald's, Gloucester 37, 38, 39, 40
St Paul's Cathedral, London 65, 66, 150
St Peter's, Barton-on-Humber, Lincolnshire 53
St Sepulchre, London 64
St Thomas of Acon, London 87
St Thomas's, Salisbury 57, 112, 114, 130
Stamford, Lincolnshire 90-1, 69
Stoke Charity, Hampshire 113, 114, 153, 161, 162, 169
Stoke d'Abernon, Surrey 47, 48
Stoke Dry, Leicestershire 116
Stoke St Nectan, Devon 45
Stourton, Wiltshire 172
Stow, Gloucestershire 87

Swanbourne, Buckinghamshire 55
Tarrant Hinton, Dorset 47
Tattershall, Lincolnshire 58
Taunton, Somerset 132, 152
Tewkesbury Abbey 72, 77, 128, 129, 147, 159, 160, 164
Thetford Priory, Norfolk 68
Thorney, Suffolk 41
Titchfield, Hampshire 169
Tiverton, Devon 99, 103, 104, 105, 108, 120
Tong, Shropshire 84, 158
Trinitarian Friars, Oxford, Oxfordshire 92
Trotton, Sussex 58
Trowbridge, Wiltshire 44
Turvey, Bedfordshire 115-6
Urchfont, Wiltshire 113, 140
Wakefield, West Yorkshire 90, 91, 92, 169
Wallingford, Oxfordshire 91
Wantage, Oxfordshire 35
Wareham, Dorset 36
Warwick, Warwickshire 84, 92, 93
Wedmore, Somerset 105
Wenhaston, Suffolk 173
West Chiltington, West Sussex 140
West Lavington, Wiltshire 116
Westminster Abbey, London 54, 63, 72, 74, 77, 78, 84, 85, 110, 124, 125, 126, 144, 156, 164, 169
Westminster Cathedral, London 178
Whalley, Lancashire 171
Wharram Percy, North Yorkshire 43, 47-8, 49
Whitby, North Yorkshire 37-8, 95, 107
Whitestaunton, Somerset 173
Wickhampton, Norfolk 58
Winchester, Hampshire
 Austin Friary 132
 Cathedral 69, 70, 72, 72, 73, 77, 120, 121, 122, 123, 124, 125, 132, 134, 137, 147, 159, 162
 College 81-3
 Hyde Abbey 35
 Nunnaminster 66
 Old Minster 41, 53
 St John's 113, 131, 137
Woodton, Suffolk 140
Worcester Cathedral, Worcestershire 70, 74, 128
Yatton, Somerset 140, 158, 165
Yaxley, Suffolk 103
York Minster, North Yorkshire 65, 150